ECONOMIC GROWTH

Economic Growth

ENGLAND IN THE LATER MIDDLE AGES

A. R. BRIDBURY

*Lecturer in Economic History
at The London School of Economics*

BARNES & NOBLE

BOOKS

10 East 53d St., New York 10022
(a division of Harper & Row Publishers, Inc.)

Published in the U.S.A. 1975 by:
HARPER & ROW PUBLISHERS, INC
BARNES & NOBLE IMPORT DIVISION

Economic Growth:
England in the Later Middle Ages
first published in 1962
by George Allen & Unwin Ltd, London

This edition first published in 1975
by The Harvester Press, Hassocks, Nr Brighton

'Economic Growth: England in the Later
Middle Ages' © A.R. Bridbury 1962, 1975

ISBN 06—490670—1

Typesetting by Campbell Graphics Limited
Newcastle upon Tyne
Printed in England by Redwood Press Limited
Trowbridge, Wiltshire
Bound by Cedric Chivers Limited, Portway, Bath

CONTENTS

ACKNOWLEDGEMENTS

I should like to thank the Town Clerks and their colleagues of Norwich, Yarmouth, King's Lynn, Exeter, Reading, Nottingham, and Leicester, for their readiness in putting at my disposal the records in their keeping. I am particularly indebted to the Town Clerk of Salisbury, Mr G. Richardson, for many kindnesses, and to the Borough Council of Salisbury for expediting my work by allowing their medieval records to be lodged in the University of London library. I should also like to thank the Secretary and Keeper of Records and his colleagues at the Duchy of Cornwall Office for turning out every scrap of medieval record that might possibly bear on my needs; the Trustees of the Leon Bequest who by appointing me to a Leon Fellowship in 1952 enabled me to embark upon the work that led to the writing of this book; the Committee of the Central Research Fund of the University of London for defraying my travelling expenses; and Miss F. M. Chandler of the Geography Department of the London School of Economics for her care in preparing the graphs.

My final debts are to two colleagues, Miss Olive Coleman and Professor F. J. Fisher, for much stimulus, and for invaluable criticism of the typescript.

NEW INTRODUCTION

When this book appeared in 1962 Professor Miller commented that it 'turned some of the current learning upon its head, making the later Middle Ages a time of economic growth and the thirteenth century a time of acute crisis for the medieval economy'.[1] In saying this Professor Miller drew attention to what is, perhaps, the main feature of the controversy that engages those who concern themselves with problems of long-term trends in the Middle Ages. It is that the controversy is not, at bottom, a controversy about the facts: it is a controversy about their meaning.

Of all the facts that bear on these problems the most important ones are those that purport to show how prices and wages fluctuated over time. No-one who has ever worked upon the records in which medieval clerks entered what we take to be the prices and wages that prevailed in the markets of particular places and periods, or who has reflected upon what has been said by those who have steeped themselves in the problems of interpretation that they raise, can be easy in his mind as to the quality or quantity of the material which everyone uses and upon which so much depends.[2] Nevertheless their trends, so far as these have been elicited from the surviving records so far examined, have been accessible to the ordinary enquirer for about a century. They are to be derived from the evidence of prices and wages recovered from the records by Thorold Rogers who was perhaps, one of the most remarkable of all the historians of the Middle Ages.[3] Statistical work

[1] E. Miller: The English Economy in the Thirteenth Century, *Past and Present*, No. 28, July, 1964, p.30.

[2] For an interesting discussion, see D.L. Farmer: Some Grain Price Movements in Thirteenth-Century England, *Ec.H.R.*, 2nd. Series, Vol. 10, No. 2, (1957).

[3] J.E.T. Rogers: *A History of Agricultural Prices in England*, vols. 1–4, Oxford 1866–82.

comparable with his goes on. But none has yet challenged his findings. And everything else that historians have done to illuminate the period from 1264, when his series began, seems to confirm the results that came out of his researches.

Yet Thorold Rogers' work dropped out of sight almost as soon as he had finished it. His volumes of figures were a mine which many historians quarried when it suited them to do so. They stirred the interest of Steffen who turned them into graphs in 1901.[4] And they were the basis for Professor Postan's remarkable analysis of population decline in the later Middle Ages.[5] But the great sweep of his work, from 1264 until the end of the Middle Ages and beyond, was substantially ignored until Professor Phelps-Brown applied statistical techniques to it with the object of displaying, graphically and in tables, what can be known at present, from his work and that of others, about changes in the purchasing power of wages through the centuries.[6] And in calculating the changes that took place in the earlier centuries, particularly in the medieval centuries for which Thorold Rogers was for long the sole authority and is still the principal one, Professor Phelps-Brown has incidentally reminded the mid-twentieth century of how much it owes to a scholar who worked in the mid-nineteenth.

For this neglect of his work Thorold Rogers was himself, perhaps, partly to blame. He lived a busy public life. Collecting data for a history of prices was only one of the many interests that occupied his time and absorbed his energies. In view of what he accomplished he should, no doubt, be excused for the use he made of

[4]G.F. Steffen: *Geschichte der Englischen Lohnarbeiter,* Vol. 1, Stuttgart 1901.

[5]M.M. Postan: Some Economic Evidence of Declining Population in the later Middle Ages, Ec.H.R., 2nd Series, Vol. 2, No. 3, 1950; reprinted in M.M. Postan: *Essays on Medieval Agriculture,* Cambridge 1973.

[6]E.H. Phelps-Brown and Sheila V. Hopkins: Seven Centuries of Building Wages, *Economica,* 1955; and Seven Centuries of the Prices of Consumables, *Economica,* 1956. Both reprinted in E.M. Carus-Wilson (ed). *Essays in Economic History,* Vol. II, 1962.

it. But the truth is that his commentary upon his findings was often at variance with them, and what he said about them on one occasion sometimes conflicted with what he said on another.[7] Even when the story he told was not subject to alteration according to the vagaries of mood or memory it was not proof against misinterpretation. What he found, and what Professor Phelps-Brown has displayed in his calculations, was that wage-earners fared very much worse 'in the thirteenth century and for most of the fourteenth, than they did at the end of the fourteenth and in the fifteenth centuries. What he said, however, was that the wage-earner did well enough in the earlier period and better still in the later one.

Until comparatively recently historians have left this apparantly trifling problem of semantics in abeyance whilst they got to work on the records of the big estates and sought to share their admiration for the way in which these estates were run with a reading public which was as eager as they were to believe that what was good for the big estates in the Middle Ages was good for everyone else. The evidence that it was not did not have to be dissembled. By common consent it was ignored. But gradually it has come to the fore, so that now it is more or less agreed that the problem of the ordinary peasant's economic circumstances in the thirteenth and fourteenth centuries is one that merits serious thought and discussion. So far, however, those who have addressed themselves to this problem have approached it from the point of view of estate records which deal mainly with the disposition of land and the obligations incurred by those who contracted to perform them. The limitations of such records are as frustrating as the difficulties of interpretation they raise. And in this rich culture of imponderables differences of opinion thrive and proliferate.[8] But one thing none of the contro-

[7] Compare *A History of Agricultural Prices* (see note 3, above) with his *Six Centuries of Work and Wages*, 1884. Conflicting comments abound in the latter volume also.

[8] The literature of the subject has been recently discussed at length in J.Z. Titow: *English Rural Society, 1200–1350*, 1969, Introduction, Section 3, *passim*.

versialists disputes: it is that the ordinary peasant of what used to be, somewhat tendentiously, called the high Middle Ages had a hard life rather than an easy one.

Does this mean that the ordinary thirteenth- and fourteenth-century peasant lived tolerably well according to his lights, as Miss Harvey appears to think he did,[9] or that retribution for the intense exploitation of the land, growing in menace from decade to decade, had already reduced him, by the end of the thirteenth century, to grinding and unremitting poverty, as Professor Postan believes it had?[10] The problem is important if we are to get the later Middle Ages into perspective. And it is, perhaps, by turning from the landed to the landless that we may best be able to tackle it.

At bottom the problem of the landless is the problem of the wage-earner. The wage-earner was not an anomaly in medieval society. Often enough he was, amongst other things, a craftsman of standing. But in over-populated rural communities wage-earning meant indispensable supplementary income for those who could not live on what they made out of their land. And wage-earning was also the last refuge of the landless before they resorted to crime. The medieval custumal concerned itself only with those who held land. Medieval law was never very strenuously exercised on behalf of the man who had no land and hence no lord. But the landless man was everywhere nonetheless. Thorold Rogers, by sticking to the custumals and following the lawyers, was able to construct a thirteenth-century rural idyll out of his records by seeing the thirteenth-century world as a world of stalwart peasant virgators.[11] But the reality his figures

[9]B.F. Harvey: The Population Trend in England between 1300 and 1348, *Trans. R.H.S.,* 5th. Series Vol. 16, (1966).
[10]*Ibid.,* p.23, note 1, for a chronological bibliography of Professor Postan's remarks.
[11]*Work and Wages,* chapters 2 and 3.

disclosed was very different. The reality was a world choked with landless men. We see them in the fourteenth century when famine and pestilence devastated the population and then returned to cut it back again and again. The immediate result was not to reduce prices as land was deserted and rents fell. The immediate result of each visitation of famine, and then of pestilence, was that things went on very much as before, and continued to do so until the last quarter of the fourteenth century. And they did so because the reserve army of landless and virtually landless men available to take up all the vacancies that occurred did not altogether dwindle away until the population had been sensationally diminished by a succession of catastrophes each one of which may very well have been more disastrous than any that medieval society had been called upon to endure in previous centuries.[12]

Nor was the wage-earner somehow isolated from the general life of the community, unaffected by the influences that dominated the fortunes of the other villagers amongst whom he lived, himself having no effect upon such influences. His standard of living may be taken as a rough and ready guide to general standards of living because there was in fact a close relationship between wage-earning and farm-tenancy. In the Middle Ages, as Professor Postan has convincingly argued, wage-earners as a class were tenant-farmers *manqués*. Only an unquenchable passion for land, indeed, can account for the way in which wage-earners forsook their employers with such disconcerting alacrity, when rents fell in the late fourteenth century, that anyone who wanted men to work for pay was thereafter obliged to offer terms which would have outraged and mortified earlier generations of employers.[13]

[12] A.R. Bridbury: The Black Death, *Ec.H.R.*, 2nd. Series, Vol. 26, No. 4, (1973). For an important discussion of wage-earning in thirteenth-century estate-farming, see M.M. Postan: The Famulus, *Ec.H.R. Supplements*, No. 2, no date.
[13] M.M. Postan: Some Economic Evidence, see note 5, above.

Consequently want and degradation in the thirteenth and fourteenth centuries could not possibly have been confined to that section of the community which devoted itself wholly or mainly to working for wages. The pressure upon space that imposed incalculable stress upon the landless was bound to have borne down upon those who occupied land by sharply worsening the terms upon which land could be acquired. If the high wages of the late fourteenth century indicated a sudden release of pressure upon space then the low wages of the previous period surely indicated that pressure had intensified. The relationship between rent and wages that Professor Postan's analysis of the late fourteenth century has elucidated, works just as well in reverse.

It is no longer self-evident, therefore, that the centuries of high Middle Ages were in fact the centuries of economic growth that they were so recently and so generally believed to be. Luxury in the midst of poverty was as abundantly in evidence in the thirteenth and fourteenth centuries as ever it was at other times and places. But economic growth is not in the least the inevitable and socially beneficial consequence of the rich indulging themselves by living luxuriously.[14] In Mandeville's world 'luxury employ'd a million of the poor'. No doubt it did as much in the thirteenth and fourteenth centuries. But it neither fed nor clothed those whom it employed so as to leave them with enough to spare for the purchase of other things—with the means, in fact, with which to stimulate the growth of the economy. Competition for work, in the high Middle Ages, cut wages to the bone, and rent drained the profits of farming from those with land, leaving wage-earners, and perhaps the majority of tenant-farmers, without enough with which to sustain life except at its lowest ebb. In such circumstances the

[14]See, for example, A.R. Bridbury: The Dark Ages, *Ec.H.R.*, 2nd. Series, Vol. 22, No. 3, (1969).

spending that was done served no better purpose than the self-aggrandisement of a class.

Can we really believe that farming was notably benefited by investment in a period when labour was so cheap and the market for farm produce so limited? The thirteenth century cannot be at one and the same time 'an age of ... technical improvements [and] the investment of capital' and also an age of 'the application of a greater amount of labour to the same amount of land', leading to 'the spread of more or less capitalistic agriculture on large estates and the consequent growth of towns, markets and mercantile classes'. The contradiction between the claim that the thirteenth century was notable for the rate at which capital was invested in the economy and also for the rate at which labour was applied to an unchanging quantity of land vitiates Professor Postan's earliest statements of what has been for long the orthodoxy of current interpretation.[15]

No-one could possibly blame the thirteenth century for failing to solve a problem of population pressure which has defeated better equipped societies than those of the Middle Ages. But it is surely difficult to admire the big estate owners for making profits when buoyant markets put money into the pockets of the most indolent of them almost as readily as they put money into the pockets of the most active and enterprising. It is even more difficult, surely, to admire them for spending so much on themselves now that it appears that they spent so little on the productive investment in farming for which they used to get so much credit.[16] And it is surely most difficult of all to admire them, as Eileen Power did, for devoting so much of the country's

[15] Professor Postan's remarks are conveniently put together in E. Miller: *The English Economy*, p.22 (See note 1, above).

[16] Dr. Titow believes that the landlords who did what they could to improve farming by investment, invested 'as much as was necessary'. Titow: *English Rural Society*, pp.49—50 (See Note 8, above). But this is a far cry from the fulsome adulation of what thirteenth-century landlords did for English farming that previous students of their activities used to express.

desperately scarce resources to sheep farming when it is clear that the wool they produced was sold abroad simply in order to pay for the food and drink, the clothes and baubles, that were imported to minister to their fancies.[17]

This change of perspective has thrown current interpretations of the high Middle Ages into disarray. Professor Postan's response to it seems to be to abjure the views of a lifetime without putting anything plausible or even coherent in its place.[18] Professor Miller is equally perplexed. He doubts whether high farming was 'a dominant feature of the whole [thirteenth] century', or indeed whether the century's expansion 'really added up to a boom' since there was 'only one potential mass market' which 'lay amongst the peasantry' whose 'purchasing power per head is likely to have fallen' at this period. And he concludes that 'the mortalities which attended bad harvest ... are hardly the symptoms of ... economic growth'.[19]

If it is now so hard to think well of the achievements of the high Middle Ages is it now correspondingly easier to think well of the achievements of the later Middle Ages? Once the scene is transformed by the removal of former constraints presumably enterprise is liberated and the big estate-owners who did so little for economic progress when they had the chance to do so much, are consigned to an unlamented limbo of historical oblivion. If none of the glamour that so recently attached to the developments of the thirteenth and fourteenth centuries can be salvaged from the ruins into which the reputation of these centuries had collapsed, then presumably the later Middle Ages must present a contrast which glows

[17] E. Power: *The Wool Trade in English Medieval History*, Oxford 1941.
[18] Professor Postan's most recent views are to be found in the *Cambridge Economic History of Europe*, 2nd edition, Cambridge 1966, Chapter 7, Section 7; and in his *Medieval Economy and Society*, 1972. For some comments on them, see my review-article in *Ec.H.R.*, 2nd Series, Vol. 26, No. 3, (1973).
[19] Miller, *op.cit.* note 1 above, pp. 32, 29, 34, 38.

ever more radiantly as preceding centuries are plunged deeper into disrepute.

But medieval historical studies are not to be so readily moved from established positions. They are still for the most part wedded to ideas about economic development which those who continue to expound them have often contributed notably to discrediting. Thus Professor Miller concedes that the later Middle Ages witnessed 'improved average consumption made possible by a reduction of people in relation to productive resources' but not much improvement in 'actual capacity to produce'. 'Increased output per head in more recent times', he explains, 'presupposes the acquisition by under-developed economies of a more advanced technology and the processes of saving, capital formation and investment which make possible its establishment'. These are the 'antecedent conditions' which he believes the later Middle Ages lacked. In their absence, he concludes, 'increased output and consumption per head are not incompatible with a cramping of the whole scale of the economy, a reduction of capital resources and a narrowing of investment and of the flow of exchanges.'[20]

It comes to this. When the peasants were starved of resources their purchasing power was diminished accordingly and this mattered because the peasant market was potentially the only mass market. When they enjoyed an abundance of resources they consumed more but still, apparently, without providing the economy with the mass market it required because the 'medieval world had a relatively limited technological equipment' which meant that 'the direct provision of consumption goods remained a prime object of a good deal of productive endeavour'. In short the medieval peasant was backward. Either he was backward because he lacked the means with which to be anything else or,

[20]*Ibid.*, pp.38–9.

when he had the means, because he lacked the knowledge.

But are we really justified in dismissing those extraordinary demonstrations of the enterprise and social aspirations of the later Middle Ages that the records discussed in the following chapters of this book so clearly depict, with the patronising and depreciatory gesture of acknowledgement which is all that Postan and Miller will vouchsafe them? The temptation to do so is strengthened, apparently, by the current vogue for referring historical problems of economic development to modern experience of societies which are what we like to call under-developed. Both Postan and Miller succumb to this temptation. But what do we know about the Middle Ages when we have called their inhabitants under-developed and compared them, without more ado, with modern communities which we also describe as under-developed? Do we know what they did or what they thought? Surely not: for only research and analysis can tell us that. And if we compare them with modern communities without further investigation how can we have the slightest confidence that we are comparing them with communities with which they have anything whatsoever in common? Is this not a travesty of the comparative method, efficacious only in the sense that it is guaranteed to solve problems without the irksome need to investigate them first, and respectable only because so many scholars are now devoted to it?

Medieval England was certainly under-developed in the sense that it lacked the capital-intensive aids to production that it acquired very much later. In that sense the most advanced economies are always more or less under-developed. But it was not primitive in the sense that its social and political organisation was rudimentary. Nor was it backward in the sense that it was an economically retarded or culturally petrified survival in a world which had left it behind as the world, including a great deal of what we call the under-developed world, has left behind so many of the peasant societies that modern anthropologists have penetrated and described and modern historians seem to have in mind when they are looking for comparisons which are implicitly disparaging of societies in the past. To say that later medieval England lapsed into a state of feckless torpor because English farmers, artisans and traders either would not, or could not, seize the opportunities they were so plainly offered, is to substitute a label for research and reflection. It is to prefer the abstract conclusions that follow from abstract assumptions to the imperfect but unequivocal testimony of the records.

But those who commit themselves to the conclusions that seem to follow from these experiments in the comparative method invite more serious trouble still. They are tempted by contemporary discussion of the problems of under-development to commit themselves to the fashionable theory that technology is the key to the secret of economic growth. Like all doctrinaire views about society this one has the irresistible appeal of simplicity. Moreover it seems to fit medieval circumstances to perfection. The whole story of medieval economic development, its false starts and inexplicable reversals, its erratic course and unsatisfactory ending, stands prophetically revealed as the inescapable consequence of technological immaturity.

But does it? The theory that economic growth depends upon technological innovation and the 'antecedent conditions' enunciated by Professor Miller is a theory and no more. What is there to be said for it? If medieval studies are not to sink into an anarchy of conflicting factions each proclaiming its monopoly of insight into the true inwardness of medieval economic conditions then its challenge must be met. And it is, perhaps, not wholly inappropriate to do so by heeding the counsel of Machiavelli who recommended that when a faith or a system is languishing the sensible thing to do is to revisit the source of its inspiration.

The source whence economic history draws its inspiration lies far back in English history, in the work of the early masters of economic thought. And there can be no question as to the place that Adam Smith occupies in that succession. *The Wealth of Nations* was published in 1776, on the eve of the greatest period of technological revolution in the history of man, and towards the end of a period when economic growth had been more rapid than ever before. The theme of the enquiry was the natural progress of opulence and its impediments. And the earliest chapters proclaimed the overwhelming importance of the growth of markets and of the division of labour in the economic advancement of society.

When Adam Smith cast about him for an example of what he meant by the division of labour he turned to pin-making, not because it was an exceptionally simple industry in which technological innovation had not, as yet, weakened the force of the lesson he was trying to illustrate, but because it was a typical one. 'In every other art and manufacture', he declared, 'the effects of the division of labour are similar to what they are in this very trifling one'.[21] And indeed everything we know about the tremendous forward movement of his age testifies to the shrewdness of his observations. In this respect, perhaps the most impressive tribute ever paid to his work is the late T.S. Ashton's *Economic History of England in the Eighteenth Century*. In Ashton's eighteenth century new methods and new tools were to be found at work everywhere. But essentially the methods and the tools used then, in farming as in trade and industry, were not new. Many, if not most, were well-tried. Never before, however, had the best of them been used so generally, or on such a scale. What had changed, fundamentally, was not knowledge but

[21] *The Wealth of Nations*, ed. E. Cannan, 1950, vol. I, p.7.

markets, not resources but the incentive to invest, not technology but the division of labour.

In what is probably the most famous aphorism in the history of economic thought Adam Smith propounded the doctrine that the division of labour is limited by the extent of the market. Medieval markets were undoubtedly limited, at any rate by later standards. Both Postan and Miller contend that they got more limited than ever in the later Middle Ages, despite their admission that ordinary people possessed, or commanded, more in the way of material resources at that time than they had done for centuries, if ever. But can this really be so? If ordinary people have the means with which to enrich themselves suddenly thrust upon them, as the ordinary people of later medieval England had, then must we not presume, if we must presume at all, that they will seize the opportunities so miraculously placed within their grasp? They may not do so. There have always been communities in which people in comparable circumstances have preferred a life of artless, if not shiftless, ease. Professor Postan thinks that later medieval England was one of these. But the presumption is very much against him. And the records tell a very different story. Nor was later medieval England a country where technological constraints upon growth persisted even when the social and economic ones had been largely removed. Professor Miller's theory is contradicted by everything that is known about the way in which English economic development took place.

Does it not follow from all this that if only we can disembarrass ourselves of views concerning the nature of under-development and theories of technologically-linked economic growth which have nothing to recommend them but their plausibility, we shall be free to recognise, in the records of later medieval England, the signs that tell of a country travelling slowly along the road to riches, by way of expanding markets and the division of labour, the road that England travelled so very much more quickly in Adam Smith's day, and that so many modern communities have travelled since?[22]

The effort to see the records unclouded by some of the fallacies of modern development theory is not made any easier, however, by recent attempts to confer upon the fifteenth-century landlord the reputation for managerial efficiency that his predecessors have so recently forfeited as a result of closer examination of what they did in the thirteenth and fourteenth centuries. Dr. Wolffe, who has examined the King's achievements in this department of his affairs during the second half of the fifteenth century, recalls problems familiar to everyone who has followed the decline and fall of the good name of the thirteenth-century landlord, by using the familiar phrases in which the virtues of the thirteenth-century estate-management used to be extolled. Edward IV, he says, created a 'new system of royal estate management' under the 'skilled professional control' of men whose families had often 'specialised in estate-management'. According to Dr. Wolffe this meant that, henceforth, the King got out of his estates not merely what he would have got out of them if wily tenants and negligent, dishonest, or incompetent agents had not deprived him of it, but also what he would have got if his agents had done everything possible to improve the terms upon which leases were granted instead of simply renewing them upon expiry without taking account of the opportunities of the case or the market changes of the time.[23]

Dr. Wolffe is dubious of attempts 'to demonstrate from specific units of estates ... that superior organisation ... was responsible for any significant increase'

[22] For a comprehensive survey of development problems see P.T. Bauer: *The Economics of Under-Developed Countries,* Cambridge 1957, and his *Dissent on Development,* 1971.

[23] B.P. Wolffe: *The Royal Demesne in English History,* 1971, pp. 160, 161, 165, 167.

of income.[24] And in fact the one example of significant increase that he ventures to offer leaves the problem where it was. The Duchy of Cornwall estates, whose income he finds substantially increased between 1433 and 1504, was worth very much more in 1504 than in 1433, not because the King's administration had improved wonderfully in assiduity in the meantime, but because half the manors of the Duchy, which had been in private hands in 1433, were restored to the crown for the benefit of the infant Duke in 1453.[25]

Dr. Wolffe's doubts about the evidence, however, would have been justified in another sense also. Not only is it difficult to find evidence to support the belief that management reforms got results: it is also difficult to believe, on the evidence, that management reforms could possibly have got results. The posthumous publication of the work done by the late K.B. McFarlane on the later medieval nobility enables us to see how little can be said for such management reforms when the most learned scholar of his generation to address himself to such matters has said everything he can in their favour.

McFarlane's view was that the nobility got richer than ever in the later Middle Ages, both individually and as a group, compensating themselves for the collapse of rents by acquiring many more of them, and by exerting themselves to get the utmost possible out of each one of their possessions.[26] But his evidence reveals a very different state of affairs. According to this, when the most exceptionally able members of the nobility had done everything they could to improve their circumstances by reforming the management of their estates, they found themselves baffled, notwithstanding, by their incorrigible failure to recruit competent or

[24] B.P. Wolffe: *The Crown Lands 1461—1536*, 1970, p.48.
[25] J. Hatcher: *Rural Economy and Society in the Duchy of Cornwall 1300—1500*, Cambridge 1970, pp. 149, 159. These manors were not alienated again in this period.
[26] K.B. McFarlane: *The Nobility of Later Medieval England*, Oxford 1973, pp. 61, 186.

reliable servants, and by their ignominious failure to collect arrears of rents that seem to have accumulated everlastingly. They issued ordinances, as did the King, and appointed commissions of enquiry. But an ordinance is wish not fulfilment; and the commissions that McFarlane cited with such approval were not so much the reports and recommendations of brisk professional executives as the lamentations of helpless participants caught up in something over which they could not hope to exercise any control.[27]

Members of the fifteenth-century nobility were not worse served than their predecessors by those that did their bidding; and they dominated the social and political world every bit as brilliantly as their predecessors had done. Indeed a noble class which keeps all the most coveted marriages firmly within the charmed circle of its own relations, and maintains an unremitting watch upon the patronage dispensed by the crown, as the English nobility did, cannot rise or fall. It can be subverted by revolution, or weakened irreparably by economic developments which nullify the commanding importance of land. Otherwise its position is always unassailable, its members, barring accidents, for ever thriving upon an unchanging round of agreeable occupations.

But this does not mean, as McFarlane apparently thought it did, that the purchasing power of noble income was somehow exempt from the exigencies of supply and demand that arbitrate at less exalted social levels. 'The greater part of the earnings of the nobility', declared McFarlane, 'was neither hoarded nor invested: it was used to achieve a higher standard of luxury.'[28] And luxury in the fifteenth century, as McFarlane very clearly showed, meant spending lavishly on service and on commodities which incorporated a very great deal of labour. But service was the most expensive thing in the

[27]*Ibid.*, pp. 213–27. One of the commissions is printed in G.A. Holmes: *The Estates of the Higher Nobility*, Cambridge 1957, pp. 126–8.
[28]*Ibid.*, p.96.

world in the fifteenth century. Whether he wanted a clerk to engross his will, or a retainer to wear his livery; whether he wanted a mason to build his country mansion or a cook to prepare his meals; the fifteenth-century nobleman had to pay more for service than his forbears and predecessors would have believed possible.

Without an income which had been very substantially increased the fifteenth-century nobleman would have been hard put to it to maintain anything like the standards of luxurious spending that his predecessors had enjoyed. Some members of the nobility un-doubtedly did manage to increase their means sufficiently to compensate themselves for loss of purchasing power. It may be that the entire nobility managed to ride out its somewhat unusual cost of living problems in this way. The small sample of noble families from whose inadequate records McFarlane got the impression that the nobility was outstandingly successful in this respect may very well prove to have justified his faith in it. But the whole class of those whose livelihood depended upon rent, the class that included the mightiest Dukes at one extreme and the humblest pensioners at the other, could not possibly have compensated itself except at the expense of labour. And to do that was out of the question because the transformation of relative scarcities, which was the determining factor in so much of later medieval economic life, had raised the exchange value of labour as decisively as the land famine of previous centuries had lowered it. This is the problem that estate manage-ment could not possibly have hoped to tackle successfully in the fifteenth century, and the reason why even the most efficient management could have done no more than minimise the losses that were bound to occur.

How these losses of purchasing power were distri-buted between the rentiers, whether the nobility gained at the expense of the gentry, which is the implication of the views expressed by McFarlane, or the gentry at the expense of the nobility, which is the implication of suggestions recently made by Professor Postan,[29] or whether indeed these abstractions can be used to tell us anything whatsoever about the social consequences of the economic changes that occurred in the later Middle Ages, are questions which cannot be pursued here. But the lesson of all these recent studies of later medieval English life is that it is fatally easy to overlook the repercussions of the revolutionary changes in the relationships of land to labour that took place at that time. No doubt it is easy to overlook something that is so big that it fills the sky, and natural, perhaps, to glance only cursorily at the social consequences of a structure of scarcities which had so brief a life-span that, in a longer perspective, it must rank merely as an interlude between prolonged periods of intense population pressure. But those who demur at the description of any period of history as epilogue, interlude, or prologue, and find the quieter tones of the later Middle Ages more to their taste than the garish splendours to which social and economic historians have generally directed their attention in earlier and later periods, must be prepared to subscribe to a trans-valuation of values such as Professor Miller deprecated in the argument of this book.[30] What Professor Miller deprecated, however, was in fact the purpose that the book was written to serve. As a contribution to an important debate it is now offered once more to those who may be interested in the problems with which it deals.

[29] See note 18, above.
[30] For the wider issues involved, see A.R. Bridbury: *Historians and the Open Society*, 1972.

LIST OF GRAPHS AND TABLES

LIST OF ABBREVIATIONS

An Old English Town: *Life in An Old English Town*, M. D. Harris, London 1898.

C.P.R.: Calendar of Patent Rolls.

Declining Population: M. Postan: Some Economic Evidence of Declining Population in the later Middle Ages, *Ec.H.R.* Second Series, Vol. II, No. 3 (1950).

D.C.O.: Duchy of Cornwall Office.

E.E.T.S.: Early English Text Society.

Ec.H.R.: *Economic History Review.*

E.H.R.: *English Historical Review.*

M.M.V.: *Medieval Merchant Venturers*, E. M. Carus-Wilson, Methuen 1954.

Prejudice and Promise: *Prejudice and Promise in Fifteenth Century England*, C. L. Kingsford, Oxford, 1925.

P.C.C.: Prerogative Court of Canterbury.

P.R.O.: Public Record Office.

Rot. Parl.: Rotuli Parliamentorum.

Seven Centuries: E. H. Phelps-Brown and Sheila V. Hopkins: 'Seven Centuries of the Prices of Consumables compared with Builders' Wage-rates', *Economica*, New Series, Vol. 23, No. 92, Nov. 1956.

Social England: *Social England in the Fifteenth Century*, A. Abram, Routledge, 1909.

Studies: *Studies in English Trade in the Fifteenth Century*, ed. E. Power and M. Postan, Routledge, 1933.

Town Life: *Town Life in the Fifteenth Century*, Mrs J. R. Green, Macmillan, 1894.

Trans. R. H. S.: Transactions of the Royal Historical Society.

V.C.H.: Victoria County History.

Work and Wages: *Six Centuries of Work and Wages*, J. E. Thorold Rogers, London, 1884.

CHAPTER I

There is perhaps no period of English history more persistently disparaged and misrepresented than the period that begins with the Black Death of 1348 and ends with the battle of Bosworth field in 1485. In retrospect it is not difficult to see how it settled into a kind of ragged unity in men's minds. The desperate vicissitudes of the years between 1348 and 1370 handed an obvious and prolific theme to monkish reproach: for the Black Death struck England with its full impact no less than three times in those dreadful years and carried off at least one-third of the population.[1] To later contemporaries there was more to these visitations than divine retribution. The Black Death was followed by the Peasants' Revolt of 1381; and in the light of that melodramatic outburst of visionary madness, and systematic violence and arson, it seemed that the Black Death had scrawled a frightful augury across the countryside. Still later observers saw these terrible events as a fitting prologue to a shameful century of regicide and civil war, public dishonour and private feud: for the House of Tudor was barely established before its friends and publicists set about extenuating the dynastic weakness of its kings, and excusing their sharp rule, by vilifying the Lancastrians and Yorkists whom they had supplanted and whose remnant they presently destroyed.

This vilification was so prodigiously successful that, even today, in the ordinary reader's mind, the later Middle Ages arouse few memories which are not haunted by the sombre drama of an annointed king dethroned and murdered, and of unhallowed successors struggling helplessly and wretchedly against the factious ambitions of unscrupulous opportunists.

[1] Declining Population, *passim*.

11

The story has now been fully told of how this myth of the Middle Ages ending politically in chaos and degradation was evolved by a succession of Tudor writers who strove to justify the present by blackening the past.[2] But no one who has read through the cycle of Shakespeare's history plays in historical order instead of in the order of writing, or who has had the opportunity to watch the unfolding of the drama of crime and punishment as Shakespeare depicted it, can doubt the real source of the enduring power of this view of the later Middle Ages.

Not that it went unchallenged. When the outstanding problem of domestic politics was commonly thought to be one of restoring and maintaining strong government, it was comparatively easy for men to agree that civil war was worse than a bad king and to point the moral of that agreement in their rendering of recent history. But when the outstanding problem was thought by many to be one of curbing the power of government, as it was in the seventeenth century, it was far less easy to get agreement. Seventeenth century writers were no less adept than their predecessors at making the past serve their turn. But whose past was it to be? The Shakespearean view of fifteenth-century treason and bloodshed as the nightmare consequences of regicide was scarcely to the taste of those who had executed Charles I. And Milton's brusque dismissal of Richard II's murder as no more than the calling to account of a wicked king had no relish for those who had sold their estates and risked their lives in the king's cause.[3]

In the long run it was individualism that prevailed, in life as in political theory: a fusion of Puritan iconoclasm and Political Arithmetic fired in the crucible of civil war. Milton's taunt flung at those who could not change their king or their government—that they 'please their fancy with a ridiculous and painted freedom, fit to cozen babies',

[2] Prejudice and Promise, *passim*; E. M. W. Tillyard: *Shakespeare's History Plays*, Chatto & Windus, 1944.

[3] *The Prose Works of John Milton.* Ed. J. A. St. John. Bohns Library. 1848. Vol. II, p. 23. See also A. Steel: *Richard II.* Cambridge, 1941, pp. 3-6.

went home.[4] And Locke's version of the theory that powers of government were only conditionally granted gave such widespread satisfaction to the propertied classes that it became at once their creed and their manifesto.

Henceforth a new note of approbation was mingled with the shrill expressions of contempt and disgust hitherto so familiar in historical writing on the later Middle Ages. Hume, in a calmer age, was able, therefore, to set a value upon the anarchy of the fifteenth century as a factor in the growth of Parliament and the forward march of liberty, without in the least depreciating its evil effects, or regarding the period, in other respects, as anything but a barbarous one when commerce was not understood and industry was shackled by meaningless regulations.

It was a point which the Whig historians of the nineteenth century did not overlook. An interpretation of English history which saw the growth of civil liberty and the evolution of representative institutions in all the major movements of the past, and in many of its misfortunes, could scarcely neglect so palpable an illustration of its theme. Lingard noted it; Macaulay, borrowing from Hallam, gave it his blessing in his brisk and cheerful way; Stubbs seized upon it and used it to justify his interest in what was otherwise 'a worn-out helpless age, that calls for pity without sympathy, and yet balances weariness with something like regrets'.[5] And J. R. Green, who was appalled by the sufferings caused by the Black Death and by the savage legislation that accompanied it; who loathed the crimes and follies of a ruling class which brought the Peasants' Revolt upon itself; who dwelt upon the miseries and want of the peasantry as depicted by Langland; deplored the fruitless waste of the Hundred Years War; turned with 'weariness and disgust' from the events of the Wars of the Roses; and condemned the literature and learning of the later Middle Ages as mere spuriousness; never-

[4] The Prose Works, as above, p. 33; R. H. Tawney: *Religion and the Rise of Capitalism*. John Murray. 1926.
[5] W. Stubbs: *Constitutional History of England*, Fourth ed. Oxford 1890, Vol. III, p. 638.

theless declared that, until then, there was never a period when the principles of constitutional liberty were better appreciated, and cited with approval Sir John Fortescue's praise of mid-fifteenth-century England as a land where monarchy was limited and law and taxation were matters for Parliamentary consent.

Green published his *Short History* in 1874. Eight years earlier, Thorold Rogers had completed his study of prices in medieval England.

This was a portentous achievement. Later scholars have strengthened it by working upon records which Thorold Rogers did not use and have correspondingly enriched and qualified it by revealing regional and local variations about which he often speculated but could not write with assurance. None, however, has yet gainsaid the trends he found, or disputed his general conclusion that the later Middle Ages were a period when the wages of peasants and artisans rose far higher than did the prices of the things they ate and drank, wore and used. Indeed looking back as far as the mid-thirteenth century and forward into periods for which he had to rely on the work of others, Thorold Rogers saw the fifteenth-century wage-earner as enjoying a standard of well-being the like of which his ancestors had never known and his descendants would never enjoy again until England ceased to be primarily an agricultural country.[6]

But if scholarship was enlarged by Thorold Rogers' findings, the perspectives of historical thinking were not. Green digested very little of what Thorold Rogers had said, though he conceded that real wages had doubled between 1349 and 1449 and acknowledged that recognition of this improvement had crept into Langland's description of the life of the peasantry. But the concession once made was soon forgotten. He praised Langland for seeing, apparently, that population growth would presently destroy this brief respite of

[6] Work and Wages, p. 522. The term wage-earner is only used for convenience. Wage-earning in the Middle Ages and until very much later was merely one of many things that ordinary people did in order to earn a living.

prosperity;[7] argued that, in any case, the wages of many labourers were high only at harvest time; and promptly returned to such cheerless but familiar themes as the mischievous truculence of landlords, the terrors of religious persecution, the horrors of the French war, and the devastating blow dealt at constitutional progress by the new monarchy of Edward IV.

Then in 1888 came the publication of Denton's history of England in the fifteenth century. This was a masterpiece of egregious perversity, depicting the later Middle Ages as a culminating period of ruinous taxation, iniquitous labour laws, demoralizing pestilences, and lavish dissipation of national resources upon violent and embittered domestic feuds and futile and indecisive foreign wars. The credulity of even the most undiscriminating reader was taxed to a degree by a portrayal in which horror succeeded upon cataclysm, in a thickening atmosphere of crime and terror, want, degradation, and wretchedness.

If Denton had ignored Thorold Rogers one might have supposed that he distrusted his methods. But Denton got up this farrago by borrowing freely from Thorold Rogers when it suited him to do so, and preferring the *obita dicta* of foreign visitors, or those expressions of Parliamentary aspiration called statûtes, when it did not.[8]

But however Green might shirk the issue and Denton cheat, the plain fact is that, for most people, in an age of violence, it is the cost not the standard of living that rises. What Thorold Rogers had done, in effect, was to propound a baffling conundrum. If the well-being of the vast majority of the inhabitants of England had improved out of all recognition in the period between the early fourteenth-century famines and the coming of the Tudors, how could it possibly have been a distracted epoch when political anarchy and private turbulence became a dominant feature

[7] The passage must be construed with a prophetic consciousness of Malthus in order to make it yield that meaning.

[8] W. Denton: *England in the Fifteenth Century*, 1888. See pp. 217-24 and Note B (pp. 311-16) for an example of his methods.

15

of social life, instead of being the casual interruption of it which they had always been hitherto?

Was it true, though, that well-being had so greatly improved? Cunningham reviewing the controversy in 1890 suggested that when the period had been more fully investigated it might very well emerge as one of general distress alleviated by the growth of clothmaking and the supplanting of alien merchants by native from English trade. The old social system was disintegrating; its successor was forming; meanwhile there was interregnum: the crown's strength had ebbed; and Parliament, though more powerful than ever once the distribution of wealth had changed, was not yet an effectual substitute for the crown in government. Wage-rates may have risen sharply in terms of the prices paid for the things most people bought. But wage-rates are not income. And Cunningham doubted whether employment was regular enough to give the wage-earner anything like the standard of living that Thorold Rogers thought he was enjoying. Indeed Cunningham believed the rates had to be high in order to compensate the wage-earner for the irregularity of the work he got.[9]

Irregular work, however, is not necessarily well-paid work, as the dock-labourers of Cunningham's day could very well have told him.[10] And wage-rates that stay obstinately high in terms of commodity prices throughout an economic system do so, not because employment is chronically irregular, but because it is impossible to attract men from other occupations without offering them a resounding inducement. Barring obstacles to movement, high wage-rates are a sort of index of contentment. And Cunningham, to his everlasting credit, though not without irreparably damaging his case, furnished the reader of other sections of his history with copious evidence of the continuing shortage of labour throughout the period.

[9] W. Cunningham: *The Growth of English Industry and Commerce.* Cambridge, 1890, Vol. I.
[10] W. H. Beveridge: *Unemployment. A Problem of Industry.* Longmans Green, 1930.

With Cunningham's work done the central problems of later medieval history entered upon a dead season of neglect. It is an unflattering reflection upon the progress of historical thinking and the development of medieval studies that for well over a generation no historian dared to venture far across the boundary dividing the 'high' from the 'later' Middle Ages, and that those bold enough to venture at all, economic historians like Ashley with the rest, scurried fearfully over the treacherous ground to the surer footholds that seemed to lie beyond.

Then in 1925 came the publication of C. L. Kingsford's fascinating portrait of England in the fifteenth century. Drawing upon private correspondence and records of litigation, Kingsford saw the fifteenth century as an age of literacy and civilization and comfort for all who kept out of politics and away from those few areas where private feuds had become violent, or where the rival dynasties fought out their quarrel during the civil war. Historically speaking, Kingsford kept better company than Thorold Rogers. His portrait was very much a portrait of middle-class, if not of proconsular felicity, with Sir William Stonor living the life of a 'country gentleman busy with the management of his estates, taking his share in the work of local administration, living in friendly intercourse with neighbours in like circumstances to himself, growing rich with his profits as a sheep grazier, and spending money on the rebuilding of his house and laying out of his garden'.[11]

Nevertheless taking them together, Thorold Rogers and Kingsford, each using quite different types of evidence, seem to have shown that England, in the later Middle Ages, despite its notorious reputation, was a country of widespread tranquility and well-being, where the institutions of law and administration, though by no means indestructible, were strong enough to withstand successive phases of weak government.

The Middle Ages culminating in Arcadian enchantment

[11] Prejudice and Promise, p. 63.

—with noises off: it was an attractive thought; but was it only a dream? So much was left unexplained. For example, Thorold Rogers said almost nothing about rent except in the sense that any history of agricultural prices is inevitably a running commentary upon the value of land. Still less did he discuss manorial profits. They were not directly his concern. He did observe, however, that the commutation of villein services for money payments had become enormously important in the early fourteenth century, at a time when famine had so thinned the population as to cause a permanent and general enhancement of wage-rates by about twenty per cent.[12]

For this observation he was taken to task; and a protracted controversy ensued to determine whether commutation was something which had taken place chiefly before or after the Black Death. The controversy had the incidentally beneficial result of producing a crop of studies of individual farms and estates that showed how profits declined, in the course of the fourteenth century, as costs rose with wage-rates and receipts fell with prices. In the end, as these studies revealed, manorial lords were forced to break up their estates into portions small enough to be taken over by the peasants. All too often they had no success in letting them, however small they made the portions and low the rents, and the countryside became a graveyard of ruinous buildings, deserted farms, and lost villages.[13]

Nor did it seem that the landlord was alone in his plight. Numerous inquiries made in the last generation or so, some into the progress of particular industries or into the development of the trade in particular commodities, others into the fortunes of certain prominent social and political institutions, appear to have yielded irrefragable evidence of the pervasive corruption and decay of later medieval society

[12] Work and Wages, p. 218.
[13] A good deal of the literature of this controversy is conveniently summarised by E. Lipson: *The Economic History of England*, Vol. I, Chapter III, A. and C. Black, 1937. See also M. W. Beresford: *The Lost Villages of England*, Lutterworth, 1954.

upon which so many previous writers had dwelt. The historian of tin-mining declared that the Black Death almost ruined the industry. If it regained its former prosperity at the very end of the fourteenth century, it did so but briefly, for 'another period of depression set in which lasted through the fifteenth century'.[14] Work on the statistics of foreign trade disclosed a sharp and almost continuous decline in the export of wool; a growing export trade in cloth that did not offset this decline in quantity and may not have offset it in value; and a steady fall in the import of wine, hitherto one of the chief imports, that became catastrophic at times in the fifteenth century, especially during the last phase of the Hundred Years War.[15] The towns, despite Mrs J. R. Green's fond esteem for them, and to her bewildered dismay, became, she thought, hopelessly oligarchic in the fifteenth century. And those who followed her into urban history discerned other signs of trouble—corporations petitioning endlessly for relief from financial liabilities on grounds of poverty,[16] swindling their M.P.s out of pay,[17] and, according to some historians, becoming so retrograde in outlook as to discourage merchants and artisans from settling or remaining where life was exposed to so many rebuffs and frustrations.[18]

If the towns had often become degenerate, so apparently had the institutions of law and government. According to Holdsworth 'by the middle of the fifteenth century, the rules of the common law were either perverted in their application or so neglected that they ceased to protect

[14] G. R. Lewis: *The Stannaries*. Harvard, 1906, p. 40.

[15] The pioneer work was incorporated in Studies; M.M.V. gives the most recent estimate of export trends, but is cautious about values. On wine see M. K. James: The Fluctuations of the Anglo-Gascon Wine Trade during the Fourteenth Century, *Ec.H.R.* Second Series, Vol. IV, No. 2 (1951), pp. 170-96.

[16] See, for example, L. F. Salzman: *English Trade in the Middle Ages*, Oxford, 1931, pp. 86-8; J. W. F. Hill: *Medieval Lincoln*, Cambridge, 1948; V. C. H. Northampton, Vol. III, p. 30.

[17] M. McKisack: *The Parliamentary Representation of the English Boroughs during the Middle Ages*. Oxford. 1932. p. 65, *et seq.*

[18] M.M.V., p. 204.

19

adequately life and property'.[19] The House of Commons, of whose independence Stubbs has been so proud, was subsequently declared to have been degraded, by this period, into a tool of baronial faction.[20] And it seemed to one authority that feudalism itself, with its stable and interlocking system of tenure and fealty, had by then dissolved into a congeries of personal allegiances, lightly given and lightly withdrawn, in which loyalty and treachery lost their meaning and conscienceless expediency governed conduct and action.[21]

The verdict pronounced by Huizinga in his famous study, *The Waning of the Middle Ages*, that the Middle Ages had dragged out their last years in gloom and decay, was thus endorsed, apparently, by every fresh piece of research that was done. It was as if Thorold Rogers and Kingsford had written about the Middle Ages of another world than the one these historians depicted.

And yet a reconciliation was perhaps possible. Professor Postan, reviewing the problem in 1939, contended that 'an age of recession, arrested economic development, and declining national income', was perfectly compatible, in certain circumstances, with a redistribution of wealth in favour of the middle classes and the peasantry.[22] Writing more fully on later occasions he juxtaposed three factors common to the later Middle Ages in order to show that such a redistribution was exactly what had taken place. Agricultural profits shrank as the margins of cultivation ceased to advance and then began to retreat without there being any increase of output per acre to compensate for the reduction of the area farmed and the accompanying fall in agricultural prices. Industrial output and profits followed

[19] W. Holdsworth: *The History of English Law*, Cambridge, 1922, Vol. II, p. 408.

[20] H. G. Richardson: The Commons in Medieval Politics. *Trans. R.H.S.* Fourth Series. Vol. 28 (1946), pp. 21-45.

[21] H. M. Cam: The Decline and Fall of English Feudalism, *History*, Vol. 25 (1940), pp. 216-33.

[22] M. Postan: The Fifteenth Century, *Ec.H.R.*, Vol. 9, No. 2 (1939), pp. 160-7.

suit, at least after the mid-fourteenth century, the cloth industry's growth, though remarkable, being insufficient to counteract the general trend. And at the same time wage-rates, in terms of the price of wheat, rose progressively throughout the economic system until early in the fifteenth century, when they reached a level they maintained for the rest of the century.[23]

What had happened, according to Professor Postan, was that famine and pestilence had caused such loss of life, and, therefore, had made land so cheap, that thousands of peasants who had formerly worked for wages could subsequently afford to farm for themselves. They did so; the supply of wage-earners fell even more rapidly than the population; and relative scarcity drove up their price.

With this conjunction of events, peasants who had become full-time farmers in their own right were as content as wage-earners who had not. Landlords, as a class, suffered grievously, as did the output of marketable agricultural surpluses: for the peasant-farmer, generally speaking, went to the market neither for labour, which the family supplied, nor for the disposal of his produce, which he and his family consumed themselves. It thus became harder to sell industrial goods; and the middle classes compensated themselves for loss of trade by organizing the closed corporations that were a commonplace of town life in the later Middle Ages, and the exclusive companies that were, by then, characteristic of foreign trade. If there were less to do, they made sure that there would be fewer to do it.

Professor Postan's views have commanded widespread acquiescence. But they have also provoked uneasiness: for England in the later Middle Ages was tremulous with change—not the dreary change traditionally associated in historical literature with the hypertrophy of old forms, in politics as in the arts, with a forlorn sense of drift, and a morbid preoccupation with death, but change that was

[23] Declining Population, *passim*; *The Cambridge Economic History of Europe*, Vol. II, ed. M. Postan and E. E. Rich, Cambridge, 1952; Some Social Consequences of the Hundred Years War, Ec.H.R., Vol. 12, No. 1 (1942), pp. 1-12.

vivid with promise and is hard to reconcile with Professor Postan's lymphatic peasants, demoralized merchants, and brutalized ruling classes which resorted to crimes of violence when they had exhausted more peaceful means of maintaining their ascendancy.

CHAPTER II

A revaluation of the later Middle Ages may quite properly begin by comparing the industrial and commercial achievements of that period with the achievements of earlier and more reputable periods. Since, however, the later Middle Ages are separated from earlier periods by catastrophic losses of population, it would be as improper to make comparisons which ignored these losses as it would be to make comparisons that ignored a revolutionary change in the value of money if that were what chiefly distinguished the later period from earlier ones.

It was Thorold Rogers who first realized that the population of fourteenth-century England began to decline, not in 1348 with the Black Death, but at least a generation before. It declined because people starved to death when the harvests failed as they did in the years 1315-17. Thorold Rogers took the rise of wage-rates in terms of corn as a rough measure of the loss; and subsequent research has confirmed and amplified his findings.[1]

This decline may have been checked in the following decade or so; but it was succeeded by colossal and unprecedented disaster when a new and intensely virulent form of plague struck the country in 1348, and returned with unabated force in 1361 and 1369. It returned again thereafter; but the shock was over. The population began to adapt itself; and the plague, though it did not cease to kill, ceased to be the sovereign determinant of the size and structure of the population that it had once been.

Not that there was rapid recovery of numbers. The fifteenth century, with its low rents and lengthening leases, was hardly an age of land hunger induced by popu-

[1] Above, p. 18; Declining Population, p. 225; and note 1; H. S. Lucas: The Great European Famine of 1315, 1316, and 1317, *Speculum*, Vol. V, No. 4 (1930), pp. 343-77.

lation pressure. And thanks to the work Professor Phelps-Brown has done on the price material compiled by Thorold Rogers and Lord Beveridge, we can be reasonably sure that the average wage-rate in the southern counties, expressed in terms of a weighted selection of commodities, doubled between the Black Death and the battle of Agincourt, held steady until about 1510, and then plunged catastrophically, falling to its lowest level for seven centuries in 1597, the year of *Midsummer Night's Dream*.[2]

Neither wage-rates nor rents are as sensitively responsive to changes in the size of the population as we could wish them to be. But as a rough guide they serve to show that, by the late fourteenth century, famine and pestilence had effectually thrust the problem of overpopulation at least four generations into the future.

Assessments of the number of people who died of plague, before its potency weakened, vary enormously. But guarded estimates of the loss of clergy in certain dioceses put it so high that one is inclined to credit the sensational losses reported in studies of particular districts and estates with more than local significance. It may well be that half the population perished. For purposes of argument, however, it will be safer to assume that no more than one-third did.[3]

Interpreted in the light of this demographic catastrophe, the industrial and commercial history of England in the later Middle Ages, far from being a sad tale 'of very slow decline, frequently arrested, but seldom reversed',[4] may prove to be, on the contrary, an astonishing record of resurgent vitality and enterprise.

There are only two sets of records complete enough for a quantitative analysis of industrial and commercial activity both before and after the Black Death. One reveals the output of tin from the mines of Devon and Cornwall in a series of accounts of the annual yield of a tax imposed at certain appointed towns upon the tin produced in the two coun-

[2] Seven Centuries, pp. 296-314.
[3] The evidence is conveniently summarized in M. McKisack: *The Fourteenth Century 1307-1399*. Oxford, 1959, p. 332.
[4] Declining Population, p. 230.

24

ties. The other tells the well-known story of the export of wool and cloth. Neither set is altogether satisfactory. The tin figures are meagre before the Black Death; the wool figures, though virtually continuous from 1280, tell of export, not of output; and the cloth figures, similarly limited in scope, are incomplete for two further reasons: native goods, other than wool, woolfells, hides, and wine, were not taxed until 1347; and before 1347 the cloth exported by aliens was not differentiated in the enrolled accounts from the cloth that aliens imported.

Notwithstanding these limitations, however, the records are a revelation. Tin production after the Black Death rarely sank much below the level of the best year for which we have evidence in the early thirteenth century. It usually compared favourably with the output recorded in surviving accounts of the early fourteenth century—an excellent time for trade when more raw wool was exported than ever before or since in recorded history. And it reached a peak at the end of the fourteenth century that had been exceeded only once before the Black Death—during the last phase of prosperity for demesne farming, the Indian Summer of the 'thirties.[5]

With a population two-thirds of its former size, England was apparently maintaining something like its former level of tin production.

In quantitative terms, the export trade in wool and in cloth was not quite so remarkable. The average annual export of wool between 1280 and 1340 was 29,374 sacks. Between 1350 and 1400, reckoning 4⅓ cloths to the sack of wool, the average export of wool, raw and manufactured, had fallen to 28,417 sacks; between 1400 and 1500, to

[5] G. R. Lewis' statement (above, p. 19), that tin production declined in the later Middle Ages, is not borne out by the statistics he printed in his Appendices J and K. Moreover, he did not print all the statistics that survive. For further details see the graph overleaf. The best early thirteenth-century year in Cornwall yielded at £2 per thousandweight, about £2,200. The total output of Devon and Cornwall is known for eight years between 1199 and 1214; the average annual yield was then only £1,700. Until the end of the Middle Ages, Devon's contribution was very small.

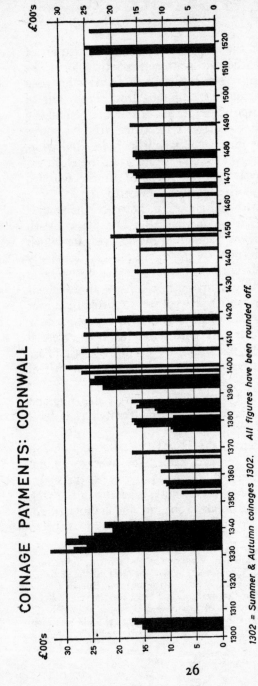

COINAGE PAYMENTS: CORNWALL

1302 = Summer & Autumn coinages 1302. All figures have been rounded off.

Sources: G. R. Lewis: The Stannaries, Camb. Harvard, 1924, Appendix K; The English Government at Work 1327-36, ed. J. F. Willard, W. A. Morris, W. H. Dunham, Camb. Mass. 1950, Vol. III, p. 92; P.R.O. E306/5/1; Sc6/812/2, 6, 7, 9, 10, 15, 18, 19, 20; 813/1, 2, 5, 8, 9, 12, 14, 22, 26; E101/263/19, 26, 28; 264/4; 266/3, 8, 13, 14, 15, 16, 22, 23. I am indebted to Mrs Stella Campbell for much help in the compiling of these references.

26

19,801 sacks.[6] A direct comparison of the first figure with the other two is not entirely fair, because the first one understates exports before the Black Death by omitting cloth. But the difference cloth would make is small, since cloth exports were probably negligible before 1330 or 1340. Consequently it is safe to say that, in quantitative terms, wool exports were virtually unaffected by loss of population until 1400, when they began to fall roughly in proportion to it.

Quantitative analysis, however, is not enough: it is value that matters. Moreover, comprehensive figures such as these obscure the remarkable changes, summarized below, that transformed the structure of the export trade in the later Middle Ages.

Annual Average	Raw Wool (sacks)	Cloth (Assize Dimensions)	Wool Equivalent (sacks)
1280-1340	29,374	—	—
1350-1400	23,973	19,249	4,440
1400-1500	10,048	42,257	9,750

Cloth was supplanting wool in the export trade. But did the substitution of a manufacture for a raw material compensate for the declining volume of wool entering into foreign trade? And how did the raw wool exported after the Black Death compare in value with earlier exports of raw wool? The problems are easier to state than to solve, because there are few things in medieval history that are more difficult to determine than the average value of these two staple exports.

In a country where the growing and marketing of wool was, for many centuries, the consuming interest of energetic farmers and ambitious financiers, the extraordinary dearth of continuous records of the prices paid for various grades of wool is at once tantalizing and inexplicable. Thorold Rogers regretted nothing so much as the poverty

[6] All the statistics of wool and cloth exports used in this book are taken from, or based upon, E. M. Carus-Wilson and O. Coleman: England's Export Trade, 1275-1547, Oxford, 1962. For the conversion rate of 4⅓ cloths to a sack of wool, see M.M.V., p. 250, note 2.

of his information about wool. Lord Beveridge, the only scholar since Thorold Rogers to make an excursion into price history at all comparable with his in range, has, so far, had no better luck. And although contemporary schedules of wool prices do survive, they are few and unsatisfactory.

The needs of medieval commerce, for example, doubtless produced a multifarious literature of mercantile sagacity. Yet only two surviving specimens bear on this problem. One is Pegolotti's handbook of the early fourteenth century; the other, an English handbook of the later fifteenth century. Both list prices of English wool. But the prices are incommensurable. Pegolotti gives two or three widely differing prices for the wool procurable from each of the monastic houses he mentions, without indicating which price relates to the bulk of the wool to be got from it. Moreover his are delivery prices in Flanders. The English handbook has a more succinct list; but its prices are delivery prices at Calais.[7]

The politics of the wool trade, so copious in their documentation, have left, nevertheless, only three schedules of wool prices. Of these, two belong to Edward III's reign— the most confused and tumultuous period in the history of wool finance.[8] And the third, though compiled in 1454, cannot be used with earlier records in order to suggest broad changes in the value of wool, if only because it is a Parliamentary petition appealing for minimum export prices in the interests of the cloth industry.[9] The majority of its prices were surely above current market prices or

[7] For Pegolotti, see W. Cunningham: *The Growth of English Industry and Commerce*, Vol. I, Cambridge, 1890, Appendix D; for the fifteenth-century handbook, B.M. MSS. Cott. Vesp. E ix, ff, 106-7. More generally, see N. Denholm-Young: *Seigneurial Administration in England*, Oxford, 1937, p. 53, *et seq.*

[8] P.R.O. C.67/22; Rymer, *Foedera*, Vol. II, pt. ii, London, 1821, pp. 1225-6. E. Power: *The Wool Trade in English Medieval History*, Oxford, 1941, p. 23, claims that there is a third fourteenth-century schedule. I have not been able to find it.

[9] Rot. Parl. V, p. 275. The petition envisaged a two-part tariff with manufacturers getting their wool at low prices and foreigners at higher ones.

there would have been no point in asking to have them enforced.

On general grounds, one might suppose that wool prices would have dropped fairly quickly after the Black Death. Sheep became relatively numerous since they did not succumb to plague; land got cheaper; and wool farming required so much less labour than arable farming that rising wage-rates could not possibly have had comparable effects on its costs.

But wool farming was not without its ancillary expenses. Flocks had to be bought and maintained, and pastures needed renewal. Moreover, the land cost at least what it was worth let. And its value let could very well have exceeded its value farmed, because the peasantry set a store by land that made it worth more than it could earn considered simply as a factor of production.

Nevertheless many landlords who had been driven from arable farming by falling prices and rising wage-rates, preferred wool farming to the alternative of leasing their estates to the peasantry. Some did so, not merely as a temporary expedient in the generation or so after the Black Death, but in the fifteenth century also. The Earls of Berkeley were still grazing sheep then;[10] officers of the Duchy of Lancaster continued to stuff certain manors of that huge estate with sheep until 1443;[11] the Abbots of Gloucester and Dorchester, Oseney and Winchcombe, sold their clips to visiting Italian merchants in the fifteenth century, much as their predecessors had done in the thirteenth century.[12] Sir John Howard, later Duke of Norfolk, no more despised the profits of wool growing in the fifteenth century,[13] than did Sir John Fastolf, sometime Major-Domo to the Regent of France.[14] Lesser county

[10] J. Smyth: The Lives of the Berkeleys, Gloucester, 1883. Vol. II, p. 7.
[11] E. Power, op. cit., p. 39.
[12] Studies, p. 52.
[13] Manners and Household Expenses of England, ed. B. Botfield. Roxburghe Club, 1841, p. 555.
[14] K. B. McFarlane: The Investment of Sir John Fastolf's Profits of War, Trans. R.H.S., Fifth Series, Vol. 7, p. 116.

families like the Stonors and the Hungerfords were content to follow where their betters led.[15] Fortescue, writing between 1468 and 1471, attributed the wealth, and hence the independence, of the yeomanry to sheep farming.[16] And Canterbury Cathedral Priory, though it did not farm any of its land by then, thought well enough of wool prices to spend £1,200 on Appledore Marsh between 1449 and 1468, and a further £300 between 1471 and 1472, in order to make it fit for leasing as sheep pasture.[17]

The activities of such wool farmers as these seem to strengthen Thorold Rogers' conclusion that wool prices varied very little between 1260 and 1400, and his strong impression that, in the fifteenth century, apart from the middle decades, average good English wool fetched much the same price as before.[18]

Thorold Rogers may very well have been wrong about the fifteenth century. His sample was small and biased. But even if average good wool fetched rather less than before, the effect of this loss of value on the export trade was probably outweighed by the gain that accrued once cloth had superseded wool as the chief export.

For cloth was worth far more than the wool it contained. A large part of its cost was the cost of the labour that went to its making. Estimates of how large a part that was are few and late. But all agree that, whether it was undyed Yorkshire cloth produced by cheap Yorkshire labour, in the late sixteenth century,[19] or undyed Essex bunting with women and girls doing the work usually monopolised by

---

[15] *The Stonor Letters and Papers*, Vol. I, ed. C. L. Kingsford, Camden Society, Third Series, Vol. 29 (1919); J. L. Kirby: *The Hungerford Family in the Later Middle Ages*, unpublished M.A. thesis, London, 1939.

[16] *De Laudibus Legum Anglie*, ed. S. B. Chrimes, Cambridge, 1942. Chapter XXIX and note on pp. 177-8.

[17] R. A. L. Smith: *Canterbury Cathedral Priory*, Cambridge, 1943, p. 203. For other examples, see *Social England*, p. 29; D. Knowles: *The Religious Orders in England*, Vol. II, Cambridge, 1955, p. 322.

[18] J. E. Thorold Rogers: *A History of Agriculture and Prices in England*. 1866, Vol. I, p. 395; Vol. IV, p. 328.

[19] *Tudor Economic Documents*, ed. R. H. Tawney and E. Power, Longmans, 1924, Vol. I, p. 217.

men, in the mid-eighteenth century,[20] the labour cost was generally half the total cost.

In the later Middle Ages labour costs were unlikely to have been less than that. Wage-rates were very high; and cloth often went abroad dyed. In the late fifteenth century, for example, something like 24,000 bales of woad were imported annually, not to speak of madder, alum, and the rarer dyes.[21] A great deal of this import was used, no doubt, in preparing cloth for the home market. But the characteristic products of important manufacturing centres with export connexions, such as York in the fourteenth century, and Bristol, Coventry, and Salisbury, throughout the later Middle Ages, were still dyed.[22]

That being so, the Table overleaf tells its own story. The first column converts average annual cloth exports into their raw wool equivalents; the second shows the raw wool being exported at the same time. By doubling the figure in the first column, so as to allow for labour costs, adding it to the figure in the second column, and deducting 10 or 20 per cent from the total in order to correct for a possible decline in the price of wool, one may get some idea of how exports in the later Middle Ages compared in value with

[20] K. H. Burley: An Essex Clothier of the Eighteenth Century, Ec.H.R., Second Series, Vol. XI, No. 2 (1958), p. 296. For other examples, see E. Lipson: The Economic History of England, A. and C. Black, 1943, Vol. II, pp. 16, 471; W. G. Hoskins: Industry, Trade, and People in Exeter 1688-1800, Manchester 1935, p. 38.

[21] This is an impression based upon the particular accounts of customs and subsidies levied at the chief ports of entry — London, Bristol, Sandwich, Southampton (P.R.O., E.122).

[22] Thus L. F. Salzman: English Industries of the Middle Ages, Oxford, 1923, pp. 209-12; Ec.H.R., Second Series, Vol. 12, No. 1 (1959), pp. 22-3; An Old English Town, p. 253; The Coventry Leet Book, ed. M. D. Harris, E.E.T.S., Original Series, Vols. 134-5, 138, 146, 1907-13, passim; Rolls of the Warwickshire and Coventry Sessions of the Peace 1377-97, ed. E. G. Kimball, Dugdale Society, Vol. 16 (1939), p. lxxvii; Salisbury Corporation Records, Ledgers A and B, passim; cloth forfeited to the aulnager, P.R.O. E.101/345/4, etc. For other evidence of cloth exported dyed, see Ec.H.R., Second Series, Vol. 12, No. 2 (1959), pp. 190-205. Dyeing was not cheap. J. S. Furley: Town Life in the Fourteenth Century, Winchester, 1946, p. 81, shows that it could be as much as 18d per 1 lb. of yarn.

EXPORTS
(Sacks)

	Cloth (Raw Wool Equivalent)	Raw Wool
1281-90		26,856
1301-10		34,493
1311-20		30,686
1321-30		25,268
1331-40		29,569
1341-50		22,013
1351-60	1,267	32,655
1361-70	3,024	28,302
1371-80	3,432	23,241
1381-90	5,521	17,988
1391-1400	8,967	17,679
1401-10	7,651	13,922
1411-20	6,364	13,487
1421-30	9,309	13,696
1431-40	10,051	7,377
1441-50	11,803	9,398
1451-60	8,445	8,058
1461-70	7,667	8,237
1471-80	10,125	9,299
1481-90	12,230	8,858
1491-1500	13,891	8,149
1501-10	18,700	7,562
1511-20	20,388	7,634
1521-30	20,305	4,990
1531-40	23,424	3,481

Note. Although all customs figures are bound to be minimum ones, it is perhaps worth mentioning that under-registration, as well as depression in trade, was probably greatest during the civil war decades of 1451-70. For an example of under-registration, see A. R. Bridbury: *England and the Salt Trade in the Later Middle Ages*, Oxford, 1955. Appendix A.

exports before the Black Death. The reckoning is, perforce, very rough and ready. But the important thing is that although the population may have fallen by one-third in the later period, the value of the export trade most emphatically had not.[23]

Nor was the buoyancy of exports maintained to the detriment of home consumption, at least in the second half of the fourteenth century; for at that period the aulnage accounts furnish a rough guide to the quantities of cloth being produced for sale at home and abroad, and show how well home consumption kept pace with foreign trade.

It is important to distinguish these accounts from later ones because, as a source, the aulnage records have long since fallen into disrepute. Aulnage was a tax paid to the crown on all cloth produced within the realm that was intended for sale rather than for personal use. It has left a profusion of later medieval records. But in 1929 Professor Carus-Wilson showed that the accounts of aulnage payment that were returned to the Exchequer could be misleading and spurious: misleading because those who presented cloth for sealing by the king's aulnager and whose names appeared in his accounts, were not necessarily those who made cloth or had it made; and spurious because, in the period 1465-78 the accounts were usually nothing but fabrications concocted by dishonest or feckless aulnagers from previous returns. So shattering was the effect of this exposure of the shifts to which fifteenth-century aulnagers

[23] H. L. Gray in Studies (pp. 7-9) estimated cloth export values (a) from customs valuations which, if not arbitrary, are at any rate very likely to be conservative, since customs men can only have had the most general notions of the cloth trade: c.f. his low estimate of wine prices, derived from the Chief Butlers Accounts (p. 14) with Dr M. K. James' far higher ones derived from more realistic sources (op. cit., above, p. 19, note 15); (b) from records of sales of cloth seized by aulnagers. Gray's sample of these was a fifteenth-century one—which is against it (see text above). And his argument that the aulnagers would try to get the best prices they could since they shared the proceeds with the Exchequer is marred by the fallacy of supposing that because someone has an excellent reason for selling to the highest bidder he has an equally good reason for returning the proceeds of his sales at their true worth.

could resort, that the work of their fourteenth-century predecessors inevitably suffered by implication.[24]

It was unfortunate that this should have been so; for the surviving accounts show that during the reigns of Richard II and Henry IV aulnagers did not simply transcribe earlier accounts, or invert lists of names to give verisimilitude to their returns, or reduce their figures to simple formulae. Dr Pelham has recently published the Warwickshire records extant for the period, and anyone who cares to do so may now examine for himself, in the pages of the Transactions of the Birmingham Archaeological Society, returns for the years 1397-8, 1399-1400, and 1405-6, which display none of the specious recurrences and rotundities that betrayed the later records to Professor Carus-Wilson's scrutiny.[25]

And by the same token, contemporary aulnagers in other important clothmaking counties such as Essex and Suffolk, Wiltshire and Somerset, were likewise innocent of the subterfuges that destroyed the value of later records and the reputation of the whole class.[26]

Moreover, evidence of the uncorrupted administration of the early aulnage system is not merely negative. No less than seven returns of Wiltshire aulnage survive for certain years between 1394 and 1415, a period when the civic records of Salisbury are fortunately very full. A comparison of aulnage with civic records shows that the men who were important in the aulnage returns were important also in the civic life of Salisbury. As they grew old their children sometimes took their places in the cloth industry, and hence in the returns, whilst they themselves might continue to be active in the service of the town. And when they died, if death overtook them before retirement, their names disappeared from subsequent returns as promptly as

[24] M.M.V., pp. 279-91.

[25] Vol. 66 for 1945-6, published in 1950.

[26] Thus Essex: P.R.O. E.101/342/9, 13, 14, 16; Suffolk: E.101/342/8, 10; Bristol and Somerset: E 101/339/2, 4; 343/28, 30; 344/3. Wiltshire: E.101/345/2, 4.

they did from subsequent records of council meetings and official business.[27]

Thus what the early aulnage returns have to say about home consumption is very likely to be somewhere near the truth. It has already been elucidated by the late H. L. Gray, the first historian to give a statistical account of the rise of the English cloth export trade. Gray used the aulnage records to assess the output and location of the industry upon which the export trade was based. In the absence of comprehensive records, he was forced to ignore the leading contribution of Norwich to cloth production, and to minimize the output of London. Moreover his estimate of mid-fourteenth-century consumption inevitably reflected the abnormal conditions that prevailed as the country recovered from the first visitation of the Black Death and before it had endured the severe visitations that were to come. Nevertheless he found that two-thirds of the cloth sealed annually in the years 1356-8 were then exported as against something like four-fifths of those sealed in the years 1392-5. Since output had increased many times in the intervening period, however, this meant, roughly speaking, that 10,000 cloths remained in the country at the end of the century where 5,000 had remained before.[28]

This astonishing growth of the home market for English cloth is not remarkable simply for the doubling, or more than doubling, of the number of cloths being sold. What makes it especially remarkable is that it took place at a period of declining population. By the end of the century,

[27]Salisbury Corporation Records: Ledger A; Domesday Books of wills proven and deeds witnessed in the Court of the Sub-Dean of Sarum, *passim*. Note especially citizens such as Thomas Eyre, John Nedler, William Doudyng, Nicholas Taillor, William Woderone, John Forest, William Warmwell, John Coscombe, Walter Nandre, Adam Teffonte, George Joce, Nicholas Harding. Unfortunately a like analysis cannot be done for other leading cloth cities for lack of parallel series of civic and aulnage records.

[28]H. L. Gray: The Production and Exportation of English Woollens in the Fourteenth Century, E.H.R., Vol. 39 (1924), pp. 13-35. As with other medieval taxation records it is for orders of magnitude that we must go to these accounts rather than for a faithful representation of the realities with which they are supposed to deal.

indeed, at least as much English cloth was being sold on the home market as Flemish cloth had once been sold there in the early years of the century, when the population was very much bigger and Flemish cloth had poured into England in unrestricted plenitude.

It is possible that the English cloth was poorer stuff than the Flemish. But this is by no means a foregone conclusion. For what reduced the Flemish import from a flood to a trickle, according to the historian of the English cloth industry, was not so much extraneous misfortune, like war or an embargo, as English competition, which stole their English markets from the Flemish clothmakers before the end of the third decade of the century.[29]

Naturally there were vicissitudes in the export of wool and cloth, during the later Middle Ages, as there were, presumably, in their output, and as there were, unquestionably, in the output of tin. But the inescapable conclusion of the available statistics of industrial production is that output per man increased so tremendously after the Black Death that, for long periods, it may have maintained the value of the total output of certain commodities at the level achieved in earlier periods of greater population — with momentous consequences for the whole social system.

These dramatic developments were accompanied by others about which, as yet, we know far less, but which probably made a substantial difference to England's foreign earnings, and hence to the command that English buyers could exercise over foreign goods and services. The merchanting of important sections of England's foreign trade, once very much the province of Flemings, and Italians, and Gascons, now passed to English control. By the end of the fourteenth century, a statutory monopoly had conferred four-fifths of the wool export trade upon native merchants, who, by a more natural evolution had, by then, largely superseded the aliens in the wine import trade also.[30] In

[29] M.M.V., p. 242.
[30] E. Power, *op. cit.*, Chapter V; M. K. James: Les activités commerciales des négociants en vin gascons en Angleterre durant la fin du Moyen Age. *Annales du Midi*: tome 65 (1953), pp. 35-48.

the course of the fifteenth century both these trades languished. But as they did so, the cloth trade grew; and aliens who had been expelled from wool and supplanted from wine, naturally sought compensation for their losses in this new and remunerative business. Here, too, however, native activity was so great that the aliens rarely managed, between them, to appropriate as much as half the exporting there was to be done.[31] And since native cloth exporters, unlike native wool exporters, usually brought cargoes rather than bills of exchange home, the decline of the wine trade was presumably counterbalanced by a switch of native interest to other goods.[32]

What the alien merchant had lost, or failed to gain, the alien shipper was unlikely to have made good. It would be chimerical to hope for a comprehensive survey to determine whether or not there was any change in the share of England's foreign trade carried in native rather than foreign ships, during the century and a half that followed the Black Death, if only because it was not until well after the Black Death that natives regularly paid tax upon all the goods they handled, and thus made a full showing in records which can be analyzed statistically. Until then they paid upon very few goods. But there are portents; intimations perhaps of greatness to come. The rise of the Canynges family of Bristol, in the fifteenth century, has been said to mark 'a new stage in the evolution of Bristol's trade. For one of the most notable features of the time is the emergence of the shipowner as a still more wealthy and influential citizen of Bristol than the merchant.'[33] If the Parliament of 1422, which Professor Roskell has so patiently anatomized, was not entirely unrepresentative of the prevailing interests of its time, then this phenomenon of the Canynges was not confined to Bristol. For, in that year, the shipowners who sat in the Commons were con-

[31] M.M.V., graph facing p. xviii.
[32] Studies, pp. 16-17. The switch may well have been to linens and canvas. See below, p. 105.
[33] M.M.V., p. 84.

37

spicuous members of that group of M.P.s whose mercantile interests Professor Roskell has been able to identify.[34]

Is it then too much to claim that the industrial prosperity of the later Middle Ages, whose progress has just been reviewed, was matched by a growth of native participation in the handling of England's foreign trade that was, to say the least of it, vigorous enough to enable native merchants to sustain the test of open competition in staple articles of commerce with those masters of the expertise of international trade — the merchants of Italy and North Germany?[35]

[34] J. S. Roskell: *The Commons in the Parliament of 1422*, Manchester, 1954, p. 53. See below, p. 98, note 32.

[35] A Navigation Act of 1381 attempted to curb alien participation in England's foreign trade; but a supplementary clause introduced in 1382 in order to modify its rigour, in fact nullified it. The next Navigation Act was passed in 1485. Lipson: *The Economic History of England*, Vol. I (1937), pp. 593-4.

CHAPTER III

From industry and commerce it might seem natural to turn next to agriculture and to investigate the later medieval fortunes of that complex group of activities. Unfortunately, agriculture, though the most profoundly important of all the economic concerns of man, is often, in its history, the most obscure. The history of English farming until comparatively recent times is substantially a history drawn from surviving remnants of the records kept by the bigger farmers. In the twelfth, and especially in the thirteenth century, these farmers, the great lay and ecclesiastical landlords of the time, kept the fullest and most splendid accounts of their enterprises to be found anywhere in medieval Europe. In the fourteenth, and especially in the fifteenth century, however, many of these landlords leased their farms, and in their accounts recorded not the bustle of the farmyard, but simply lists of the rents paid by the tenants to whom they had surrendered their lands.

The tenant-farmer was no newcomer to the English country scene in the later Middle Ages. He had an intricate and ramifying lineage which, in a sense, embraced the villein who paid his rent chiefly in services and dues, as well as the more conventional leaseholder and tenant at will who paid their rents in cash. But it was in the later Middle Ages that he began his familiar and unrivalled domination of English agriculture. And since he kept few records of his costs and receipts, if indeed he kept any, and these, such as they were, have carried badly, it was then that a new darkness fell upon our knowledge of how the land was farmed.

A position which will not yield to direct assault, however, can sometimes be turned. What matters about later medieval agriculture, for the purposes of this essay, is not how it organized the growing of crops and the rearing of animals; what matters is whether it prospered or not. And prosperous or depressed, self-sufficient or commercialized, later medieval agriculture cannot have failed to exert the most powerful influence upon the towns; for towns being in the highest degree embodiments of specialization of function are incomparable registers of the ebb and flow of economic life.

In the later Middle Ages, as at all times, towns were generally speaking no less productive than farms or workshops, though their products were more various and included the provision of services as well as the making of things. They were in no sense parasitic on the countryside —the self-indulgence of an affluent society. Their main business was to release farmers from having to market their own produce and turn their own raw materials into finished goods. In doing this they in fact raised the quality of the goods and services available by making manufacture and distribution their full-time concern. In short, towns were indispensable components of the economic system. No economy has ever advanced far without them. To study them is to study the entire system at a vital confluence of flows.

The following three chapters will be devoted, therefore, to an analysis of the scraps and shreds of evidence from which the story of their later medieval vitality may perhaps be pieced together.

English medieval towns are usually depicted in terms of mingled enthusiasm and regret—enthusiasm for the years of obvious growth, when new towns multiplied and old ones expanded; and regret for the later Middle Ages, when, with some exceptions, they are thought to have dwindled, through poverty and neglect, into huddles of ramshackle and derelict buildings where sinister gangs fought over trifles amidst the encroaching grass, their governing bodies, so recently the proud and liberal exemplars of democracy, now degenerated into wolfish oligarchs, whose characteristic posture, in addressing the king, was a rapacious cringe, and in dealing with ambitious inferiors, a truculent patrician swagger.

The independent conclusions of many different but converging lines of investigation make this account less a travesty of historical opinion than a composite portrait of what is generally looked upon as a waning institution. The constitutional historian, fascinated by the emergence of towns from a feudal countryside, found them more interesting, and perhaps, by an unconscious equivocation, more active, whilst they struggled towards independence by wringing concessions from necessitous landlords, than when they were fully emancipated, and there was nothing for him to do but describe their incorporation and watch them enjoying their triumph.[1] The political historian, writing under the spell of romantic medievalism cast by William Morris, and, in this context at least, still unbroken, saw something like universal suffrage in such phrases as 'the consent of the whole community', when they occurred in records of the acts of town governments in the twelfth and thirteenth centuries, and a hardening towards autocracy in later rulings that confined elective and legislative powers to fewer than one hundred citizens.[2] The Parliamentary historian, delighted to find burgess politicians thronging the assemblies called together by Edward I, his son, and grandson, noted that urban interest in national politics declined in the reign of Henry IV, if not before, when non-resident lawyers and the country gentry began to infiltrate into urban constituencies, and that by the midfifteenth century it was probably the exception rather than the rule for towns to pay the salaries of their M.P.s in full.

[1] M. Weinbaum: *The Incorporation of Boroughs*, Manchester, 1937.

[2] C. W. Colby: The Growth of Oligarchy in English Towns, E.H.R., Vol. V, 1890, pp. 633-53; *Town Life, passim; Records of the Borough of Leicester*, ed. M. Bateson, Cambridge. Introductions to Vols. I (1899) and II (1901), *passim*; J. W. F .Hill: *Medieval Lincoln*, Cambridge, 1948, pp. 276-7, etc.

The age of the carpet-bagger and the rotten borough was at hand.[3]

The most telling evidence of urban distress, however, was marshalled by local historians using petitions drafted by conniving lawyers on behalf of corporate clients and addressed in abject and importunate terms to the king, imploring him to reduce a fee-farm rent, or remit a tax, which it was no longer within the capacity of loyal but destitute citizens to pay. The desperate misfortunes recounted in these petitions ranged from dramatic and unexampled losses caused by fire and flood, foreign attack, and piratical affray, to the insidious and stultifying effects of excessive taxation, the silting up of a harbour, costly litigation, and competition—always unfair competition—which was driving crafts into decline and citizens into exile.[4]

Looking forward to the third and fourth decades of the sixteenth century, certain local historians have invoked the public health acts which were passed then to show that there was nothing transitory or fortuitous about the decline of the towns. Acts requiring the corporations of towns with tumbling buildings, and dangerous or noxious streets, to clear and rebuild them in the interests of safety and hygiene, were incompatible, so it seemed, with urban prosperity and that becoming sense of municipal pride and self-respect which prosperity should engender. And scarcely any of the major towns escaped nomination in one or other of these Acts.[5]

More recently, the fortunes of English towns in the later Middle Ages have been assailed from another quarter. Professor Carus-Wilson has argued that the widespread adoption of fulling mills tilted the balance of advantage against the town, as the principal location of the cloth industry,

[3] M. McKisack: *Parliamentary Representation of English Boroughs during the Middle Ages*, Oxford, 1932, p. 61; V. C. H. Wilts, Vol. IV, p. 78.

[4] A good deal of the evidence has been marshalled by Salzman, see above, p. 19, note 16.

[5] Statutes of the Realm 27 Hen. VIII c.1; 32 Hen. VIII c.18, 19; 33 Hen. VIII c.36; 35 Hen. VIII c.4.

42

and in favour of those country districts, in the west and the north, where cloth workers could combine the benefits of fast water for milling with freedom from urban taxation and gild control. And the undeniable difficulties encountered by clothworkers, during the early fourteenth century, in cities such as Winchester, Oxford, Lincoln, York, London, Northampton, and Leicester, which had once been leading centres of clothmaking, seem to add irresistible force to her conclusions.[6]

Thus a formidable consensus of opinion supports the view that most English towns declined in importance, shrank in size, and dwindled in prosperity, for a period beginning in the early fourteenth century to which it is impossible to set a term in the Middle Ages, and even, perhaps, in the sixteenth century.

Yet an economic system whose chief mining and industrial products enjoyed so ample a measure of prosperity as English tin and cloth apparently did in the later Middle Ages, could scarcely do without towns. Industrial production, indeed, has particular need of an urban environment. Whether it be the cloth industry of the fourteenth century, or the cotton industry of the eighteenth, all the stages of manufacture, except perhaps for finishing, were carried on most efficiently when they werc carried on in fairly close proximity to one another, and to the innumerable subsidiary trades upon which they all depended.[7] Transport, merchanting, building, engineering in wood as well as in metal, ample supplies of raw material, labour, and capital, available when they were needed, and not before or after— these and scores of other services industry required then as

[6] M.M.V., Chapters IV and V.

[7] D. Defoe: A Plan of the English Commerce, 1728. Reprinted Blackwell 1928, pp. 63-4; T. S. Ashton: An Economic History of England: The Eighteenth Century, Methuen, 1955, pp. 95-6. For other examples, see W. G. Hoskins: Industry, Trade and People in Exeter, 1688-1800, Manchester, 1935, p. 53, et seq.; K. H. Burley: The Economic Development of Essex in the later Seventeenth and early Eighteenth Centuries, unpublished Ph.D. thesis, London, 1957; K. J. Allison: The Wool Supply and the Worsted Cloth Industry in Norfolk in the Sixteenth and Seventeenth Centuries, unpublished Ph.D. thesis, Leeds, 1955.

it does now. And where they were to be found together, from an industrial point of view, that place was a town.

How then is this apparent conflict of evidence and reason to be resolved? Was the industrial prosperity of the period such that the towns could accommodate it within the compass of a greater decline? Or was there something exceptional about the medieval cloth industry that enabled it to flourish outside the towns, despite the patent inconveniences of a country setting? Or is accepted historical opinion wrong?

To some extent the problem is a result of narrowness in the definition of what constituted a town in the Middle Ages. Tempers have been shortened, and arteries hardened, in the vain quest of a way of isolating those essential attributes of a town that all can recognize but none can define.[8] Into these coterie wrangles we need not intrude. From an economic point of view a place should be reckoned as a town, rather than a village, not when it satisfies some abstract legal or constitutional notion of borough status, but when more than a tiny minority of its inhabitants can earn a livelihood by devoting their working hours to the manufacturing and servicing industries rather than to farming.

All classification of social institutions is bound to be arbitrary at the point where differences are small, a classification by division of labour no less than any other. How, for example, is one to determine the status of an urban district like fifteenth-century Stroudwater, where settlement was too scattered for the area to rank as a town, and industrial interdependence between the villages so complex as to make nonsense of their separate identities?[9] But such a classification at least has the merit of recognizing the true worth of such fifteenth-century clothmaking centres as Lavenham and Hadleigh which, though they were villages in legal and constitutional theory, had far better claims to

[8] James Tait: *The Medieval English Borough*, Manchester, 1936.
[9] E. M. Carus-Wilson: Evidences of Industrial Growth on Some Fifteenth-Century Manors, Ec.H.R., *Second Series*, Vol. 12, No. 2 (1959), p. 190, *et. seq.*

be called towns than any number of chartered boroughs which returned members to Parliament and paid at the urban rate the tax on moveable property of 1334.[10]

The problem of reconciling industrial expansion with urban decline cannot be solved, however, simply by calling the bigger clothmaking villages, town; for the aulnage records show that, by the end of the fourteenth century, no less than one-third of all the cloth marketed in England was brought for sealing to aulnagers working in the regional capitals of Salisbury, Bristol, Coventry, and York.[11] The loss of the Norwich returns, though unfortunate, is not irreparable, since the magnitude of the Norwich contribution can be roughly estimated from other sources. So great does this contribution appear to have been that, with it, the aulnage records might very well have put the share of the regional capitals in the sealing of cloth at something approaching three-fifths.[12]

The cloth sealed in these cities was not all made there. Professor Heaton, using the Yorkshire accounts, has described the weekly procession of small clothmakers who hurried their cloths and half-cloths from the surrounding villages into Leeds and Bradford, Wakefield and Halifax, to get them sealed and sold as soon as possible.[13] And some of the Bristol accounts are detailed enough to show that village clothmakers were as active in the neighbourhood of a big city as they were in the neighbourhood of small Yorkshire towns.[14] Silas Marner, suitably transposed from linen to woollen weaving, was no fiction. He was a recognizable type.

[10] B. McClenaghan: *The Springs of Lavenham*, Ipswich, 1924; G. Unwin: *Studies in Economic History*, Macmillan, 1927, Chapter VII, Part (1). Below, Appendix III. See also K. C. Newton: *Thaxted in the Fourteenth Century*, Essex Record Office, Chelmsford, 1960, for an interesting example of a village on the threshold of becoming a town.
[11] H. L. Gray: The Production and Exportation, p. 32 (cited above, p. 35, note 28).
[12] See below, pp. 49-50.
[13] H. Heaton: *The Yorkshire Woollen and Worsted Industries*, Oxford, 1920, p. 71.
[14] M.M.V., p. 290, and note 4; also *Town Life*, Vol. II, p. 105, note 2.

Indeed clothmaking had no sooner become a marketable skill rather than an indispensable domestic virtue, than it was turned to profit by country people who went on combining it with farming as they always had done, but now produced a saleable surplus instead of restricting their output to their personal needs. Since it was not their only means of livelihood, they could presumably afford to compensate for their comparative inaccessibility by charging less for their work than urban craftsmen did, and perhaps, in favoured districts, by using mechanical aids like fulling mills to make their costs competitive.[15] Moreover, the closer they lived to the urban centres of the industry, the easier it was for them to lower their costs by taking advantage of the commercial and industrial facilities these places could offer them. This surely is the significance of the numerous villages in Somerset, on either side of the Stour in Essex and Suffolk, in Berkshire, and even in Yorkshire, whose appearance in the late fourteenth-century aulnage returns Gray hailed as a sign that clothmaking had 'burst the bounds of medieval town life'.[16]

Nor was this all that village labour did for commercial clothmaking. The work of preparing the raw wool and spinning it into yarn required so much more labour than later processes, such as weaving, that it often had to be

[15] This remark is not intended to imply that fulling mills were only used by those on the fringes of the industry. They were undoubtedly in general use and profoundly affected location, though large centres of production like Bristol and Salisbury seem to have managed almost without them. (Bristol and Gloucs. Archaeological Soc., 1886, *passim*, and Vol. 66 (1945), pp. 61-7; Salisbury Corporation Records: Ledgers and Wills, *passim*). But they did not apparently take the industry out of the towns: simply to better sited ones. To this conclusion Professor Carus-Wilson's thirteenth-century evidence is not an obstacle (M.M.V., Chapter IV). At that period of falling wages labour-saving devices were the last thing industry needed. Fulling mills, like ovens, wine-presses, and corn-mills, were installed by landlords simply as a means of screwing additional sums of money out of their tenants. Hence their economic effect must have been to raise, not to lower, the costs of thirteenth-century rural clothmaking.

[16] Gray, *op. cit.*, pp. 30-32.

done in villages scattered about the hinterland of a town as a constellation is about its sun.[17]

Nevertheless it would be wrong to credit the villages of medieval England with more than a small share in the commercial production of cloth. New towns, in the sense of ancient settlements grown complex, accounted for very much more.[18] But it was the established boroughs, many of them places of antique privilege and importance, that made the largest single contribution of all.

The aulnage accounts are perfectly clear about this. The commercial output of villages and small towns, whenever there was much of it to record, was distinguished from the output of the big towns. As new centres of clothmaking sprang up, the aulnagers added them to their lists. In Yorkshire, during the fifteenth century, they added Halifax, and Bradford, and Professor Heaton has indicated how abundantly they were justified in so doing.[19] In Wiltshire, before 1414, the aulnagers arranged their accounts under two headings—Salisbury, and the county. Thereafter they distinguished the separate contributions of Wilton, Devizes, Castlecombe, and Mere.[20] And from recent work in manorial history, we can appreciate that they did so because places like Castlecombe had, by then, expanded industrially to the point at which it is a nice problem to decide whether they were still villages, or had become small towns.[21]

The aulnagers seem to have recognized the growth of new centres of clothmaking so readily that one can scarcely account for the importance they ascribed to the big regional capitals except on the assumption that most of the cloth they sealed in these capitals was actually made there rather than elsewhere.

But we do not have to be satisfied with assumption. A

[17] *Town Life*, Vol. II, p. 105.

[18] Gray is content to go on calling these places villages.

[19] Heaton, *op. cit.*, pp. 71, 75-6, 93, refers to medieval wills without actually citing examples; see also V.C.H. Yorks, The City of York, p.90.

[20] P.R.O. E.101/345/2 and 4.

[21] Carus-Wilson. Evidences of Industrial Growth, cited above, p. 44, note 9.

profusion of evidence survives which confirms that cloth-making played a dominant rôle in the life of some of the largest provincial cities of later medieval England. The streets of York and Bristol, Norwich and Coventry, are a palimpsest from which the marks left by the medieval cloth industry have not been quite rubbed away.[22] Scores of the convey-ances of medieval Salisbury bear witness to the tenter-yards for the stretching of cloth that were set up in convenient places all over the city and even across the Avon in Fisher-ton which, by the late fourteenth century, was being rapidly absorbed into the industrial life of the city.[23] It is impossible to study the council minutes and the bye-laws of these five cities without being struck by the incessant practical con-cern of their civic authorities with every aspect of cloth-making.[24] Lists of their civic dignitaries testify to the vitality of even the humblest textile crafts, by showing that weavers and fullers could occasionally rise to the highest positions without first renouncing all connexions with their crafts.[25] And when trouble brewed, and the town clerk could be bothered to set down the names of all the craftsmen who attended the extraordinary meetings then held, his records vouchsafe a fleeting glimpse of how large these groups of urban textile workers could sometimes be.

Such a meeting was held at Salisbury on February 5, 1421, when the town clerk entered in the city's ledger the names of some 400 weavers and fullers who met to consider the grave consequences of the king's decision that their striped cloth must conform to the statute of measures,

[22] The present names of streets and closes are abundant evidence of this.

[23] Salisbury Corporation Records: Domesday Books, passim; The Tropenell Cartulary, ed. J. Silvester Davies, Devizes, 1908, Vol. I, p. 170, et seq. Tenters were called racks in medieval Wiltshire.

[24] The Records of the City of Norwich, ed. W. Hudson and J. C. Tingey, Norwich, 1910, Vol. II, passim; Salisbury Records: Ledgers A and B; York Memoranda Book, ed. M. Sellers, Surtees Society, Vols. 120, 125 (1912-14); York Civic Records, ed. Angelo Raine, Vols. I-II; Yorkshire Archaeological Society, Vols. 98, 103 (1939-41); The Little Red Book of Bristol, ed. F. B. Bickley, 1900; The Great Red Book of Bristol, ed. E. W. W. Veale; Bristol Record Society, Vols. IV (1933) and VIII (1938).

[25] See below, pp. 58-9.

despite their demonstration, with the help of three cloths, one raw, one partly fulled, and one completely fulled, that such cloth could not be 6 quarters wide.[26] According to the Poll Tax returns of 1377, Salisbury then had 3,226 lay inhabitants aged 14 and over.[27] At least half of these were women and girls; and some of the men were probably incapable of work. Consequently unless Salisbury's population had grown prodigiously between 1377 and 1421, weaving and fulling, to say nothing of the other textile processes, clearly occupied at least some of the time of a very large proportion of its active male citizens.

The evidence of admissions to the freedom is equally compelling. Annual lists of these admissions survive in continuous series for very few medieval towns. Fortunately Norwich and York have theirs. The Norwich lists, however, omit the craft affiliations of so many freemen admitted before the reign of Henry IV that they are impossible to interpret before then. But subsequent entries leave no doubt as to the immense importance of clothmaking to Norwich. Average decennial admissions show that between 19 per cent and 28 per cent of all those admitted to the freedom in the fifteenth century chose to be admitted as members of the textile crafts—as weavers, fullers, dyers, cardmakers, shearmen, and the like.[28] The York lists are detailed and continuous enough to provide a comprehensive survey of admissions from 1311 until the end of the Middle Ages. They show that admissions to the freedom by way of the textile crafts rose from 2 per cent to 15 per cent of all admissions between 1331 and 1371, and were

[26] Salisbury Corporation Records: Ledger A, fols. 43 and 72, dorso.

[27] J. C. Russell: *British Medieval Population*, Albuquerque, 1948, pp. 142-3.

[28] *Calendar of the Freemen of Norwich, 1317-1603*. Compiled J. L'Estrange, ed. Walter Rye, London, 1888. Average annual entry into the textile crafts was as follows:

1401-10	7	1451-60	10
1411-20	8	1461-70	6
1421-30	7	1471-80	4
1431-40	6	1481-90	4
1441-50	7	1491-1500	8

never less than 12 per cent between 1371 and 1401, and between 1441 and 1471. At other periods of the fifteenth century they fluctuated between 8½ per cent and 11 per cent.[29]

The York figures are unusually interesting because York was a city to which clothmaking was inevitably a subordinate concern. The seat of the northern province of the Church, the capital of the north, and to judge by the admissions, an important centre for the manufacture of armaments, particularly when there was war with Scotland,[30] York was the focus of activities so very much more varied and notable than those of other provincial towns that its citizens' predilection for the clothmaking crafts is all the more impressive.

Craft affiliation, though not an infallible guide to what a man did for a living in the Middle Ages, is unquestionably a suggestive one. An aspirant to the freedom too poor to join one of the mercantile crafts that ran the towns of medieval England might easily have elected, for personal or accidental reasons, to become a weaver, rather than a carpenter, a smith, or a baker. But when many aspirants, over a long period, preferred the textile crafts to the building, metal-working, or catering ones, then it is likely that their preference had some larger significance than personal fancy or the luck of the draw. And this is particularly so when the towns whose freedom they aspired to enjoy are known from other records to have been greatly concerned with the marketing, if not with the making of cloth.

There was, of course, nothing to prevent those who joined what purported to be manufacturing rather than mercantile crafts from occupying themselves chiefly with the selling rather than with the making of cloth. Certainly

[29] J. N. Bartlett: The Expansion and Decline of York in the later Middle Ages, Ec.H.R., Second Series, Vol. 12, No. 1 (1959), pp. 22-3. The number of York freemen that elected to enter the freedom by way of the textile crafts was not much greater, in this period, than the number that so elected at Norwich. For York's cloth output, see Gray, above, p. 35, note 28.

[30] V.C.H. Yorks. The City of York, passim.

those who made, often sold as well. The crisis that threw the Salisbury cloth interests into confusion in 1421 was caused, specifically, by the confiscation of striped cloth which had been taken to the Westminster Fair in 1411 by 'makers of cloth' whose names, enrolled some months later by the town clerk, sometimes reappeared in 1421, when a plenary session of weavers and fullers met to discuss what was to be done about the king's decision not to sanction the customary dimensions of Salisbury cloth.[31] But, on the whole, a man with means enough to live by buying and selling would sooner or later transfer to a mercantile craft rather than resign himself to lifelong membership of a subordinate group whose other members could scarcely be more than piece-rate workers.[32] Those few who prospered and did not so transfer, sometimes retained their interest in manufacture throughout life; for their bequests show that at death they still had in their possession the instruments and raw materials of their craft.[33] It was a whimsical choice, though valuable to the historian, since it provides yet more evidence that the big cities were important centres for the manufacture as well as for the marketing of cloth.

[31] Salisbury Corporation Records: Ledger A, fol. 43.

[32] *Town Life*, Vol. II, pp. 121-2; M.M.V., Chapter V.

[33] Bristol and Gloucs. Archaeological Soc. (1886); Salisbury Corporation Records: Domesday Books, *passim*; P.C.C., Marche 5 (Stylle), Marche 21 (Eyre), Luffenham 3 (Shirley), Logge 1 (Swayne), Dogett 1 (Briggys); V.C.H., Yorks. The City of York, p. 88.

CHAPTER IV

The making and marketing of cloth may have added substantially to the prosperity of a certain number of English towns in the later Middle Ages. But they sustained very few at their pre-Black Death size. Indeed the vacancies and dilapidations that are commonplaces of so many late medieval account rolls of corporate property show that towns, by then, had plenty of room to spare. In the circumstances it could hardly have been otherwise. Town populations had to be fed. But the farming community, being much smaller after the Black Death, would have found it extremely difficult to support as many townspeople as before without a revolution in farming methods or help from abroad.

There was no help from abroad: corn imports were meagre throughout the later Middle Ages.[1] Average physical productivity per acre, however, certainly rose. As land got cheaper farmers shifted from the least accessible sites and the poorest soils, to richer and more rewarding ones. This, as Professor Postan has pointed out, is surely the lesson of the contradictory evidence about the effects of the Black Death that manorial historians have adduced in support of their conflicting claims: the Black Death caused greatest disruption on the worst farming land and least change, at any rate in the short run, on the best. And as leases lengthened, with far greater security of tenure, farmers very likely took a great deal more care of their land than they had ever done hitherto.[2]

But as labour became relatively scarce and land relatively abundant, it was productivity per man that increased rather than productivity per acre. Falling rents meant that

[1] N. S. B. Gras: *The Evolution of the English Corn Market*, Harvard, 1926, Appendix I B.
[2] Declining Population, pp. 241-2. For the leases see below, p. 90.

the average peasant holding, and hence average peasant productivity, probably increased as dramatically after the mid-fourteenth-century pestilences as we know they did in Ireland after the mid-nineteenth-century famines.[3] As long ago as 1900, Miss Davenport demonstrated how falling rents had enabled the peasants of Forncett manor in Norfolk to add acre to acre, in the course of the later Middle Ages, and thus to carve substantial farms from the manorial estate.[4]

Miss Davenport's example was necessarily an isolated one, and later research has done little, unfortunately, to generalize her conclusions. But if we cannot be certain that peasant productivity, in the later Middle Ages, was most commonly increased by the enlargement of peasant holdings, what we cannot doubt is the growth of that productivity. The rising trend of wage-rates and the falling trend of corn prices bear unequivocal witness to it. For without it the low corn prices would have spelt poverty for all farmers of arable at a time when there were high wages to be earned in other occupations, and worse than poverty for anyone who attempted to farm his arable with hired labour. In such circumstances the ordinary peasant-farmer might have resigned himself to doing most of the work on his farm with no more assistance than his family could render him, and to accepting low returns as his lot. Many men, in all ages, have preferred a life of overwork as their own masters to one of material ease as other men's servants; and such is the attraction of the land that the ordinary peasant-farmer might very well have felt that the sacrifice of income was worth the price. His sons, however, and particularly his younger sons, who had fewer expectations, were unlikely to have shared these feelings; sooner or later

[3] Ireland, Industrial and Agricultural. Department of Agriculture and Technical Instruction for Ireland, Dublin, 1902, p. 305, et seq; Journal of the Statistical and Social Inquiry Society of Ireland, Vol. 18 (1950-51), pp. 459-61; The Great Famine, ed. R. D. Edwards and T. D. Williams, Dublin, 1956.

[4] F. G. Davenport: The Decay of Villeinage in East Anglia. Trans. R.H.S. N.S. Vol. 14, 1900. See also her book: The Economic Development of a Norfolk Manor, Cambridge, 1906.

they would have left; and their drift from slogging and unremunerative work at home to well-paid work elsewhere would inevitably have forced corn prices to rise as their withdrawal from arable farming caused output to fall, and wage-rates to fall as their entry into wage-earning occupations caused the supply of labour to rise.

Increasing productivity doubtless went some way towards compensating for the diminished labour force that could be devoted to the feeding of the towns. But this was not the only factor affecting their size. The towns lost their power to draw people from the countryside as the land recovered its attraction for them. The destruction of life by famine and disease had transformed the ordinary farm-labourer's prospects. Hitherto, especially in the late thirteenth century, pressure of population on rural resources, which, to judge by the upward movement of rents and corn prices, were not increasing quickly enough to give them a livelihood, had forced many farm labourers to look elsewhere for employment. Unfortunately for them the population crisis was accompanied by an intensification of feudal tyranny: customary rights were abridged, customary obligations redoubled.[5] Villeinage therefore immobilized an important class of tenants and made it very difficult for heirs in villeinage to move. But younger sons, and members of other classes, were not similarly impeded by feudal covenants, and had every inducement to evade their trammels. The records are full of their journeyings. Mostly they gravitated to the towns where life was so complex that they might hope for sufficient work to maintain themselves and their families.

In the towns, however, ordinary migrants were denied access to the most coveted and profitable opportunities by legislation which confined unenfranchised labour to work that was unskilled, or at best, semi-skilled. Accordingly they were forced into jobs to which entry was virtually free, and in which employment was fluctuating and uncer-

[5] M. Postan: The Chronology of Labour Services, *Trans. R.H.S.*, Fourth Series, Vol. 20 (1937).

tain. Unskilled work, free entry, fluctuating employment: it was the formula that Mrs Sidney Webb found working with such deadly effect in the London docks towards the end of the last century, where many more were attracted to the available work than could get a decent living from it, and few achieved more than what was, in effect, outdoor relief.[6] Can we seriously believe that the formula worked less effectually in the thirteenth century than it did in the nineteenth; or doubt that thirteenth-century towns were not so much populated as swollen and choked with people, all hoping for the living that the countryside could no longer give them, and all but a few hoping in vain?

After the mid-fourteenth-century pestilences, however, the land, far from having more people to support than resources with which to do it, suddenly had more resources than people. Stock, equipment, buildings, land of every description, were suddenly scarce no longer; only labour was hard to come by. The peasants seized their unprecedented opportunities, despite the strenuous efforts the landlords made to stabilize wages and conditions of service by getting statutory authority for their needs in 1351 and special courts in which to enforce them. There was land for all, work for all, hope for all, and the peasants were not to be thwarted: the Revolt of 1381 with its culminating scene of a boorish mob dealing in terms of disrespectful menace with the anointed king, was at once a warning of a new mood and an earnest of resolute purposes.[7] The lesson was not lost upon those whom it was intended to instruct, and, in the long run, conditions of feudal tenure were relaxed as landlords adapted themselves to the new realities of life and were glad to get tenants on any terms rather than not at all.

Henceforth, therefore, the towns could continue to recruit labour from the countryside only by exerting a more positive attraction than that of being refuges for the workless. But it was no easier for townsmen to adjust their

[6] W. H. Beveridge: Unemployment. (Above p. 16, note 10.)
[7] B. Wilkinson: The Peasants' Revolt of 1381, *Speculum*, Vol. 15, No. 1 (1940), pp. 12-35.

outlook to changed circumstances than it was for landlords. Past experience was no guide whatsoever to future conduct. For past experience was dominated by memories of constitutional triumphs, many of which were achieved in the thirteenth century, when landlords who were importing a new stringency into their relationships with the peasantry, were nevertheless driven, or encouraged by economic prospects, to confer upon burgage tenure that privileged status which they enshrined in the charters for which the period is famous.

These charters did not enfranchise all who dwelt in towns. The community of which they spoke was the community of the elect.[8] Sometimes they specified the group to which their privileges were to be confined.[9] Often, as Professor Carus-Wilson has taught us, they conferred commercial and industrial monopolies upon one class of citizens whilst explicitly denying them to others.[10] Nor was the burgess status that seemed to vouchsafe admission to the charmed circle easy to acquire: it normally entailed the satisfaction of arduous conditions and the payment of fees.[11] Fugitive villeins were by no means enfranchised by mere residence, though residence might free them from the fear of being reclaimed.[12] Accordingly the rights of burgesses were a jealously guarded monopoly of the few, and the transactions of town councils show how promptly persons were prosecuted who presumed to exercise them without having 'made their entry'.[13]

[8] A clear case is that of Lincoln where it was stated that the fullers had no community with the citizens. M.M.V., p. 237, note 5.

[9] The clauses granting quittance from tolls are usually the most revealing ones: they confine the privilege to certain groups such as members of the Merchant Gild. British Borough Charters 1216-1307, ed. A. A. Ballard and J. Tait, Cambridge, 1923, p. 254, et. seq.

[10] M.M.V., p. 223, et seq.

[11] See, for example, the introduction to The Register of the Freemen of Leicester 1196-1770, ed. Hen. Hartopp, Leicester, 1927.

[12] Records of Nottingham, ed. W. H. Stevenson, 1882, Vol. I, pp. 3, 9, cited by Lipson in his Economic History, Vol. I, p. 218, but misconstrued by him. See also C. Gross: The Gild Merchant, Oxford, 1890, Vol. I, p. 70.

[13] Thus The Records of the City of Norwich (cited above, p. 48, note 24), Vol. I, p. xxxiv.

Yet in the conditions of the thirteenth century their chartered privileges gave towns, if anything, an added appeal: towns could offer, not only the chance of work, but also a prospect of freedom, however distant that might be for many. The thirteenth century was a period therefore when the ruling burgesses could stand out for almost any terms they cared to impose upon those who sought the sanctuary and the prizes of town life.

That their terms were exceedingly rigorous is hardly in doubt. And it would be hard to find a more striking example of their ruthless exercise of the power that circumstances and privilege had placed in their hands, than their universal practice of debarring all members of the gilds of weavers and fullers from their councils, and thus, in effect, turning them into second-class citizens.[14] The mortified pride and stifled ambitions of these and other lesser citizens made a treacherously unstable compound which exploded when national problems were brought to issue in mid-century. Baronial discontent, crystallizing under the leadership of Simon de Montfort, was accompanied by widespread urban insurrection. And from the things said then and later it is evident that the lesser citizens of very many towns were being forced to bear the brunt of the taxes levied by ruling burgesses who nevertheless kept all the powers of government to themselves.[15]

The records, though meagre, indicate moreover that these lesser citizens were by no means always non-burgesses. Since it was usually taxation that turned restiveness into turbulence, grievances stressed the means rather than the status of petitioners. But it is reasonably clear that those who controlled the towns sometimes managed, by force perhaps, if not by chicanery of one kind or another, to oppress fellow-citizens who, in name at least, were no less enfranchised than they. At Oxford in 1255, for

[14]M.M.V., p. 223, et seq.

[15]Authority for the facts in this and the next paragraph are to be found in E. F. Jacob: Studies in the Period of Baronial Reform and Rebellion 1258-67, Oxford, 1925, pp. 118-19, 136-7; V.C.H., Northants., Vol. III, p. 7.

example, the protests against the outrages perpetrated by the greater burgesses came from 'burgesses of the lesser commune' as well as from the poor. This threefold classification of citizens was very common in the thirteenth century. Hence it is possible that the 'middling' and 'secondary' citizens of other towns whose protests have found their way into recorded history were also burgesses, and not unenfranchised artisans and tradesmen calling themselves middle-class to avoid being confused with the poor. If they were, then oppression of fellow-burgesses was a regular feature of thirteenth-century town life. Oligarchic power could hardly go farther than that.

When times changed, however, the towns were equal to their challenge. Contrary to prevailing notions in historical circles, the structure of urban society in the later Middle Ages became, not less flexible, but more so. It was a remarkable achievement for bodies whose thirteenth-century tradition of oligarchy sprang, it seems, from an even earlier tradition of hereditary aristocracy.[16]

Their response was not merely a negative one. It was not simply that governing bodies became less glaringly unrepresentative of the citizens over whom they presided because there were fewer to rule over as total numbers fell. Two positive changes were made: members of the gilds of weavers and fullers were admitted to the freedom and thus given their chance of rising to the highest positions that civic life could offer; and governing councils were enlarged.

It is impossible to say when the new trend in admissions started. Surviving lists of admission are few, often late, and as a rule, tantalizingly negligent in recording the crafts of new freemen. But several towns were clearly admitting weavers and fullers in the early fourteenth century. York, whose register begins in 1272, seems to have started admitting them in 1319, just as the country was recovering from

[16] A. B. Hibbert: The Origins of the Medieval Town Patriciate. *Past and Present*, No. 3 (1953), pp. 15-27; G. A. Williams: London and Edward I, *Trans. R.H.S.*, Fourth Series, Vol. 11 (1961), pp. 81-99; V.C.H., Yorks., The City of York, pp. 46-7.

the appalling famines of 1315-17.[17] Norwich and Colchester, with lists dating from 1317 and 1327 respectively, were certainly admitting them by then.[18] And Leicester, whose thirteenth-century record of exclusion Professor Carus-Wilson has made notorious, began to atone for it at least by 1334, when the first of many members of the town's weaving and fulling community, of whose craft we can be sure, entered the Merchant Gild and became a fully-enfranchised citizen.[19]

For some, this emancipation was only the first step. Wherever the records are full enough, we can see that weavers and fullers sometimes rose to the top. York had a mayor who was a weaver in 1424[20]; Northampton, eight bailiffs who were either weavers or fullers in the period 1386-1461[21]; Coventry, a bailiff who was a weaver sometime before 1449[22]; Salisbury, numerous senior citizens, in the later Middle Ages, members of one or other of these crafts, whose opinions told in council and whose public service helped to make local administration work.[23]

If they appear to be few who achieved the highest positions as members of these crafts, the reason, as suggested before, is usually that ambitious business men were rarely content to keep humble company when they could afford the company of those who were influential and distinguished. Consequently ambitious weavers and fullers usually transferred to the wealthiest and most prominent group that would accept them. Indeed in some towns, such

[17] *Register of the Freemen of the City of York*, Vol. I, ed. F. Collins, Surtees Society, Vol. 96, 1896, pp. 18-19.

[18] *Calendar of the Freemen of Norwich* (cited above, p. 49, note 28); *The Oath Book or Red Parchment Book of Colchester*, ed. W. Gurney Benham, Colchester, 1907.

[19] *Register of the Freemen*, as above, p. 56, note 11.

[20] Thomas Bracebrigg: see J. N. Bartlett's unpublished London Ph.D. thesis (1958): *Some Aspects of the Economy of York*, pp. 90-91.

[21] V.C.H., Northants., Vol. III, p. 28.

[22] *An Old English Town*, p. 275.

[23] Thus Salisbury Corporation Records: Ledger A, *passim*: cf. the lists of weavers and fullers with the members of the 24 and 48 and of special commissions empanelled from time to time.

as Norwich, where a citizen could not take office unless he belonged to one of the leading crafts, special arrangements were made for candidates from other crafts to change their craft membership, though not necessarily, as in the thirteenth century, their business.[24]

As to the enlargement of governing bodies, again the trend is unmistakeable. At Norwich, where a council of 24 dominated the town in the thirteenth century, there was, by 1415, an additional council of 60 with powers of veto over the 24.[25] Lincoln, with an equally small council in the thirteenth century, had a 12, a 24, and a 40, by the early fifteenth century.[26] Leicester and Northampton, each ruled by a 24 in the thirteenth century, promoted an Act of Parliament in 1489, in order to reduce the crowds that thronged election meetings, that secured for them governing structures of which the main elements were a 24 and a 48.[27] King's Lynn, again with a 24 in the thirteenth century, acquired another council, this time a 27, by the early fifteenth century.[28] York, dominated by a small group of family dynasties in the thirteenth century, had acquired, by the late fourteenth century, a government controlled by merchant princes in which more representative elements were nevertheless important.[29]

These additional bodies, on paper at least, were not all equally powerful. Some were elected indirectly and presumably could have been packed; though even packed they had the rudimentary merit of giving the lesser citizens a small share in government where their predecessors had had none. In practice, however, the contrast with the thirteenth

[24] The Records of the City of Norwich, Vol. II, pp. 289-90 and l-li. For thirteenth-century practice, see M.M.V., p. 234.

[25] The Records, as above, Vol. I, pp. lxviii-lxix.

[26] J. W. F. Hill: Medieval Lincoln, Cambridge, 1948, pp. 261, 276-7, 301-2.

[27] V.C.H., Northants, Vol. III, p. 9. Presumably the 24 and 48 were fewer than had become customary earlier in the century.

[28] Town Life, Vol. II, p. 419, et seq. See also J. Tait: The Medieval English Borough, Manchester, 1936, pp. 280-81.

[29] V.C.H., Yorks., The City of York, pp. 46-7, 77-8.

century could scarcely have been greater. The special circumstances of particular towns varied so much that all generalization runs the risk of being impaled upon an exception. But, on the whole, what is impressive about minutes of council meetings in the later Middle Ages is not their evidence of the despotism of exclusive juntoes. What is impressive about them is their revelation of the extraordinary care taken by civic authorities to consult the wishes of the burgess community at large whenever important decisions were pending. Normally it was hard enough to get a quorum: at Salisbury and King's Lynn, for example, more than one council meeting had to be abandoned for want of a minimum attendance. But critical issues brought the burgesses flocking, there and elsewhere. Thus at Lincoln, in 1422, some 200 named burgesses assisted at one meeting; in 1438, 96 burgesses assisted at another.[30] At Coventry, 91 'worshipful persons' discussed the reception of Queen Margaret in August 1456; and in 1472, during the dispute over the Lammas lands, 153 named, and many more unnamed burgesses, were asked to express their wishes so that the council might know what to do.[31]

These are very large numbers. Their true significance only the surviving lists of admissions to the freedom can suggest. Unfortunately these lists are not all they might be. Very few are continuous enough to be useful; and each has its special deficiencies. York's list has the fewest, being all but unbroken from 1272. But the lists extant for Norwich, Colchester, and King's Lynn, are all more or less meagre for the period before the Black Death, Colchester's having the added drawback that, after the third or fourth decade of the fifteenth century, it ceases to record the names of new burgesses who had been born in the town. Exeter's list, though apparently excellent, may very well under-register admissions, particularly in the fifteenth century, during

[30] J. W. F. Hill, as above, pp. 276, 278.
[31] *The Coventry Leet Book*, ed. M. D. Harris, E.E.T.S., Original Series, Vol. 135 (1908), pp. 285, 376-7.

the constitutional struggle between the town and the Tailor's gild; and Leicester's, though it starts earliest of all, is wanting for the period 1380-1466.[32]

Despite these serious shortcomings all but one of these admissions lists show important towns in several regions of England admitting each year, on the average, as many burgesses in the century following the Black Death as they had done before it. York's record, indeed, is especially remarkable: between 1351 and the end of the Middle Ages, York for long periods admitted twice as many burgesses as it had ever done since its surviving admissions records began.

This even succession, or better than even succession, to the burgess ranks conceals a momentous change in the structure of urban society. No one who cares to make a comparison between the topographical evidence for town growth in the thirteenth century, and the testimony of one series of rent rolls after another as to the impossibility of letting corporation property in the later Middle Ages, will doubt for a moment that most provincial towns had many fewer inhabitants after the Black Death than before it. Consequently what the admissions lists show is that the proportion of burgesses to other citizens of all degrees rose sharply in certain towns after the mid-fourteenth century.[33]

Loss of record makes it impossible to know how widespread this change was, or what delays there were, as perhaps there were at Exeter, before it took place. If there is any consolation for this tantalizing check to our knowledge, it is surely that, since the records we still possess survived by accident, there is no reason to suppose that the trend they reveal was exceptional.

Scrutinized more closely, these lists are even more reveal-

[32] The lists for York, Norwich, Colchester, and Leicester, have been printed and are cited above. The King's Lynn and Exeter lists are still unprinted. For the Exeter struggle, see *Town Life*, Vol. II, Chapter VII.

[33] Perhaps less sharply at York than elsewhere, since the population of York seems to have recovered more rapidly; see Bartlett: The Expansion and Decline of York, pp. 24-5 (cited above, p. 50, note 29).

ing: for burgess numbers were not maintained simply by making entry easier than before. Entrance fees were not lowered in the later Middle Ages. On the contrary, in some towns, such as Oxford, they were much increased.[34] Nor were burgess numbers maintained merely as a consequence of admitting weavers and fullers. At York and Norwich, two exceptionally important centres of clothmaking, weavers and fullers were, at most, 14 per cent and 20 per cent respectively, of all new admissions. There was not even a great deal of entry by patrimony, that is, by exercise of the right of a freeman's heir to take up the freedom without apprenticeship, and often, without fee. The Exeter, Colchester, and York admissions, which distinguish those who entered by patrimony from the rest, show how very few availed themselves of that privilege. And what Professor Thrupp and Dr Hoskins have taught us about the brevity of burgess dynasties makes it unlikely that these records, though few, are unrepresentative or seriously misleading.[35]

In short, all the evidence points to apprenticeship as being the normal method of entry. And apprenticeship meant, usually, seven years' virtually unpaid probation. Seven years when wage-rates are low may be no great hardship. Indeed, in the circumstances of the thirteenth century, few opportunities were harder to come by, or more prized, than those to which apprenticeship was the indispensable qualifying preliminary. But seven years in the later Middle Ages meant a very considerable sacrifice of income, not only because the rates paid to skilled men were then very high, but also, and more particularly, because the differences between the wage-rates commanded by the skilled and the unskilled had become comparatively slight.[36] It was, in fact, not simply income that was being

[34] H. E. Salter: *Medieval Oxford*, Oxford, 1936, p. 46.

[35] S. L. Thrupp: *The Merchant Class of Medieval London*, Chicago, 1948, Chapter V; W. G. Hoskins: English Provincial Towns in the Early Sixteenth Century. *Trans. R.H.S.*, Fifth Series, Vol. 6 (1956), pp. 9-10.

[36] *Work and Wages*, Vol. I, pp. 233, 236-7; W. Beveridge: *Wages in the Winchester Manors*, *Ec.H.R.*, Vol. VII, No. 1 (1936).

sacrificed by the later medieval apprentice: it was easy money, with no call being made for special aptitude, or knowledge, or training.

Town life was obviously offering something very worth while for it to be able to attract and hold so large a community of burgess tradesmen and artisans when other opportunities beckoned as temptingly as the wage-rates suggest they did.

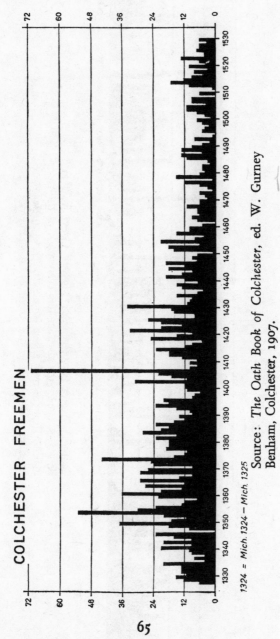

COLCHESTER FREEMEN

1324 = Mich. 1324 — Mich. 1325

Source: *The Oath Book of Colchester,* ed. W. Gurney
Benham, Colchester, 1907.

E

65

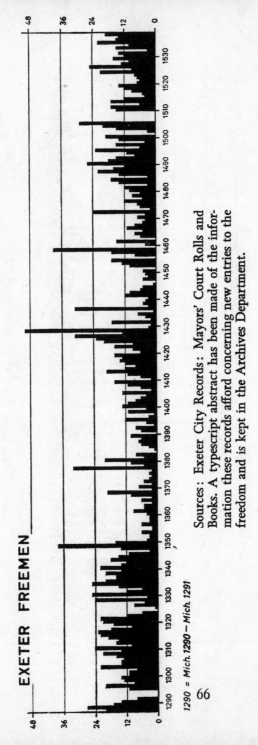

EXETER FREEMEN

1290 = Mich. 1290 − Mich. 1291

66

Sources: Exeter City Records: Mayors' Court Rolls and Books. A typescript abstract has been made of the information these records afford concerning new entries to the freedom and is kept in the Archives Department.

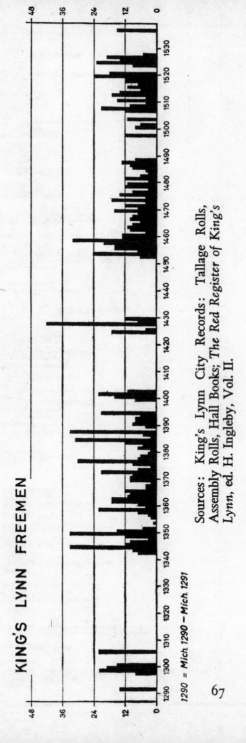

KING'S LYNN FREEMEN

1290 = Mich. 1290 – Mich. 1291

Sources: King's Lynn City Records: Tallage Rolls,
Assembly Rolls, Hall Books; *The Red Register of King's
Lynn*, ed. H. Ingleby, Vol. II.

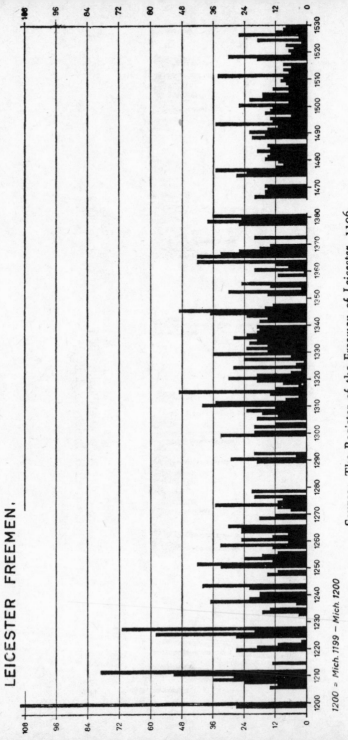

LEICESTER FREEMEN.

1200 = Mich.1199 – Mich.1200

Source: *The Register of the Freemen of Leicester, 1196-1770*, ed. H. Hartopp, Leicester, 1927.

68

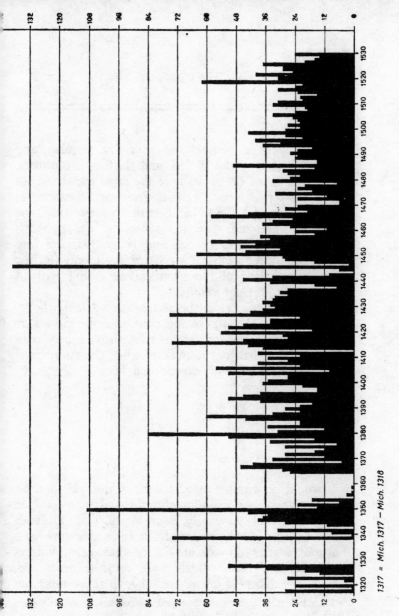

1317 = Mich. 1317 – Mich. 1318

Sources: *The Calendar of the Freemen of Norwich,*
1317-1603, compiled by J. L'Estrange, ed. Walter Rye,
London, 1888; with corrections by W. Hudson and J. C.
Tingey, for which see their *The Records of the City of*
Norwich, Vol. II, Norwich, 1910, Introduction, *passim.*

CHAPTER V

The astonishing growth of towns in size, number, and complexity, during the twelfth and thirteenth centuries, was an inevitable concomitant of the rapid expansion for which the period is well known. Professor Beresford has found evidence for the foundation of no fewer than 109 new towns between 1100 and 1300; and although few throve as New Salisbury did, and many dwindled into villages, or wasted away, to survive, if at all, only in their ruins, the phasing of these foundations is not without interest to the present inquiry.[1]

The great majority, as the accompanying table shows, were founded between 1150 and 1250; while no more were founded in the latter half of the thirteenth century than during the first half of the twelfth, when the disorders of Stephen's reign had made expansion difficult:[2]

1100-50	21
1151-1200	31
1201-50	36
1251-1300	21
1301-70	6

It would be wrong to read too much into this decline, and after 1370, total cessation of new foundations set upon land which had previously been agricultural. Professor Beresford's necessarily restricted definition of a new town must not be allowed to obscure the fact that ancient villages could, and in the later Middle Ages, not infrequently did, grow to the stature of towns, even though at law none was

[1] I am indebted to Professor Beresford for permission to use figures which he feels are still only provisional.

[2] M. Postan: Glastonbury Estates in the Twelfth Century, *Ec.H.R.*, Second Series, Vol. V, No. 3 (1953), pp. 358-67; *ibid.*, Vol. IX, No. 1 (1956), pp. 106-18.

recognized as being in any way different from what it had been formerly. Nor did the growth of the economic system depend upon the evolution of new towns even in this wider sense: existing towns could very well cope with more business simply by expanding.

Nevertheless the decline of new foundations after 1250 coincided with those circumstantial expressions of urban discontent voiced by middling and poor citizens about which something has already been said. Feudal law and population pressure, by causing an excessive concentration of labour in the towns, had undoubtedly given urban oligarchies exceptional opportunities for oppression. Their evident success in exploiting these opportunities, however, and in enforcing harsh restrictions on commercial and industrial enterprise, is hard to reconcile with accepted notions of the later years of the thirteenth century as a period of confident and energetic growth. For although merchants are often supposed to conspire unceasingly against the public interest, it is usually in hard times, not good, that they succeed in closing ranks, restricting entry, and limiting production; and they succeed because it is in hard times, when risks are greatest, that they have a common interest to share between them whatever business there is to be done.

The later thirteenth century was certainly a period of rising agricultural prices and profits. But it was also a period when the steady worsening of the ordinary peasant's conditions of life was so widespread as to imply a general failure of agricultural and industrial development to keep pace with mounting numbers. The trouble was that although the farmers could undoubtedly have expanded the output of corn by cultivating poorer and more intractable soils, by cultivating more intensively, and by diverting land from other uses, they could have done so only by incurring greater costs and therefore by charging higher prices. To some extent that is what they did. But as population pressure forced the earnings of labour to fall, they found that the prices that would give them a fair return on their investments were higher than most people could afford to pay. The expansion of the output of corn, not for the last time in history, thus became least attractive at the moment of greatest need.[3]

This did not mean, however, that rents necessarily ceased to rise. On the contrary, arable farming being only one use for land among many, there is every likelihood that the hitherto inexorable advance of rents continued almost unchecked. Sheep, for example, devoured men in the thirteenth century much as they did in the sixteenth; and the sportsman with his forests and parks was perhaps no less an enemy of corn production than they. Rising rents, moreover, enriched those who wanted, not rudimentary things like a subsistence diet and the barest shelter from the weather, but palatial homes, exotic imports, stately churches, personal services, and the like. Thirteenth-century England, with the ever-deepening plight of the mass of its peasantry, and the lordly ostentation of its ruling classes, was plainly threatened with the fulfilment of the gloomiest prognostications of the classical economists.[4]

From the mercantile point of view rent had become a sort of all-consuming behemoth, first reducing the market for manufactures by leaving ordinary people with very little money for anything but food, and then leaving them with scarcely enough even for that. Nor were there compensations elsewhere. The beneficiaries of this trend, land-

[3]It is difficult to explain the medieval failure to raise output by applying the simple techniques known then but only used widely later, except in terms of the failure of effective demand.

[4]N. Denholm-Young: Seigneurial Administration, passim (cited above, p. 28, note 7); J. R. Strayer: The Laicization of French and English Society in the Thirteenth Century, Speculum, Vol. 15 (1940), pp. 76-86. Recent work on population pressure has only served to strengthen a view of the thirteenth century that sees the wretchedness of the peasantry as one of its dominant features. Thus: M. Postan and J. Titow: Heriots and Prices on Winchester Manors, Ec.H.R., Second Series, Vol. XI, No. 3 (1959), pp. 392-411; J. Titow: Some Evidence of the Thirteenth-Century Population Increase, ibid., Vol. XIV, No. 2 (1961), pp. 218-23; H. E. Hallam: Population Density in Medieval Fenland, ibid., Vol. XJV, No. 1 (1961), pp. 71-81.

lords and others with tolerable security of tenure, did not hoard their accumulating wealth. But spending it brought scant relief to other classes. With population in spate, fierce competition for work kept profits and wages low, whilst rent entered ever more deeply into the cost of food and raw materials, and handed control over the resources of the economy ever more fully to those who received it. The culminating phase of demesne farming in England, for all its vaunted achievements, was in fact, for the majority, something of a Ricardian nightmare; and the mercantile classes, reacting sharply, took such measures of self-defence and mutual aid as circumstances permitted.[5]

The restrictions they then enforced so sedulously were never subsequently annulled. Nor was the machinery of gild inspection upon whose prompt and vigorous use so much depended, later dismantled. But town records of the later Middle Ages, though on the whole much fuller than those surviving from earlier periods, give the impression that these restrictions were invoked far more rarely then than before, and that the emphasis of legislation had passed from problems of industrial control to problems of public hygiene and public safety.[6]

Even the fullest medieval records of urban life are meagre compared with what is available for the study of more recent periods, and impressions can very easily be mistaken.

[5] The wave of mercantile bankruptcies that yielded the evidence of early fourteenth-century poverty cited by Professor Carus-Wilson may be partly explicable in these terms (M.M.V., pp. 204-6); as may be the banishment of the Jews.

[6] To some extent this change of emphasis was a result of the emancipation of weavers and fullers, which disposed of a whole range of possible infringements of regulations. To some extent it was a result of the transfer of a good deal of industrial control to the Sessions of the Peace. See *Proceedings Before the Justices of the Peace*, ed. B. H. Putnam. Ames Foundation, Harvard, 1938, Introduction, *passim*. But even in these courts indictments for infringements of statutory limitations on terms of service were few, owing perhaps to collusion between employers and employees. See *Rolls of the Warwickshire and Coventry Sessions*, p. lxxvii (cited above, p. 31, note 22). Rural practice may have differed from urban, it being far harder for farmers who were getting low prices for cereals to pass on higher labour costs than it was for manufacturers who were getting comparatively high prices.

But a change of emphasis was not unlikely at a period when hitherto disfranchised classes were being emancipated, constitutional reform was giving lesser citizens a rôle, if only a minor rôle, in the government of the towns, and burgess ranks were relatively fuller than ever before.

Naturally it is impossible to generalize about a country as intensely localized as England then was without doing injustice to regional diversity. Not all towns were equally liberal in their reforms; nor were they all less populous after the Black Death than they had been before it. London is the outstanding exception to nearly all generalizations about later medieval towns. A strong case has been made out for the swift recovery of York from the ravages of the Black Death, the subsequent decline of its population being delayed until the fifteenth century.[7] And there may have been other towns with similar experiences of recovery followed only later by loss of numbers.

It is easy, however, to make too much of regional diversity. The more localized life is, the fewer are the opportunities for specialization, and the more uniform is the pattern of activities likely to be. What the evidence adduced in the last chapter strongly suggests, is that, generally speaking, urban life was much easier in the later Middle Ages than it had been in earlier times. And if restrictionism is the product of adversity, this greater ease creates a presumption that towns, and hence the countryside, were more prosperous then than before.

Loss of numbers is no bar to this conclusion. Indeed if the great size of many thirteenth-century towns had been a sort of elephantiasis caused by poverty and the workings of feudal law, then loss of numbers may very well have been more of a boon than a misfortune.

[7] See above, p. 50, note 29. York was certainly a smaller place in the fifteenth century than it had been in the late fourteenth century. It may very well have been a poorer place also. But it would be wrong to compare York before the Black Death with York at any time in the fifteenth century and declare that the fifteenth-century city was a shadow of its former self without first taking into account the nation-wide demographic changes of the period.

The loss undoubtedly entailed lower rents, falling property values, and, in so far as municipal revenues were based on the rating of property, declining corporate incomes. Of this decline the towns made all the use they dared; consequently their petitions and importunities cannot possibly be taken at face value. Bedford, for example, secured from Henry VI a remission of over half its annual farm, mainly because it declared that the town's rents could no longer support the old farm.[8] An admission as damaging and illuminating as this was unusual; but the habit of assigning revenues to the servicing of a particular debt, and then pleading poverty when these revenues dwindled, may very well have been common, and should not be construed to mean that the towns were always as poor as they would have the king think.

Moreover this was far from being the only kind of deception to which medieval municipalities resorted. It is now nearly seventy years since Mrs J. R. Green drew attention to the chicanery that enabled towns like Coventry and King's Lynn to conceal their immense wealth from the king by transferring balances from their civic treasuries to their Gild Merchant accounts, or by accumulating funds there whilst incurring vast deficits in their civic treasuries.[9]

Naturally enough their deficits never hindered the towns that practised such imaginative and profitable departures from the orthodoxies of public finance from rebuilding or embellishing their halls, and market-places, and other civic property, in the fifteenth century, or from repaving their streets as many towns then did.[10] Nor did they

[8] C.P.R. 1445-52, p. 36, cited, for example, in the Exchequer Pipe Roll for 1524-5: P.R.O. E. 372/370.

[9] Town Life, Vol. II, pp. 216, 406, 410-11.

[10] Coventry: M. D. Harris: The Story of Coventry, London, 1911, Chapter XVI; An Old English Town, pp. 87, 92, 359. Norwich: Records, Vol. II, pp. xxxv-ix, lxxi, cxxix. Bristol: M.M.V., p. 4; W. Hunt: Bristol, Longmans (1895), pp. 105-6. York: J. N. Bartlett, see above, p. 59, note; V.C.H., Yorks, The City of York, p. 107. Colchester: G. Martin: The Story of Colchester, Colchester, 1959, p. 35. Northampton: V.C.H., Vol. III, pp. 36, 41, 45, 47, 48-9. Leicester: V.C.H., Vol. IV, pp. 342, 358, 361, 367. Oxford had six colleges before the mid-fourteenth

quench the flow of civic and personal generosity whenever there was a chance that making loans to the king might benefit the town or its citizens.[11]

And even when there was every justification for a plea of poverty it does not in the least follow that the citizens who entreated so pathetically for the reduction of civic burdens such as the farm, and the moveables tax, were as straitened personally as they may have been corporately.

Unfortunately nothing is harder to estimate realistically than the worth of a class of persons whose wealth consisted mainly of stocks of goods, raw materials, and debts, and whose probate inventories have long since perished. Even outlay upon buildings is no guide: for the houses of thriving merchants, unlike palaces and churches, unless they happen to survive long enough to be treasured as precious memorials of ancient and undying civic traditions, or to share the extraordinary fate of John Hall's mansion at Salisbury, which lives on transmogrified into a cinema, generally make way for roomier and more comfortable structures as soon as a generation appears which can afford them.

But the quest for evidence that the mercantile classes were rich when they claimed to be poor, must not be allowed to obscure the larger purpose for which the evidence is required. If the social and constitutional changes described in previous pages do, in fact, imply a growth of urban prosperity in the later Middle Ages, then what is really needed is evidence that urban wealth formed a larger proportion of total wealth in the fifteenth century than it did in the thirteenth.

Since Clio is a muse, and therefore wayward with her

---

century and acquired New, Lincoln, All Souls, and Magdalen, by 1448. Cambridge also had six before 1350, acquiring a further seven by 1500. Furthermore many colleges, in both universities, founded before 1350, received some of their greatest benefactions later or did much of their finest building later: Merton's library is late fourteenth century. V.C.H., Vol. III, for both counties. For the repaving see Social England, p. 17; G. T. Salusbury: Street Life in Medieval England, 1948, Chapter I, passim.

[11] See Appendix I.

favours, the historian with his special problems must, perforce, accept philosophically whatever indulgence she may extend to him. If it is impossible to assess changes in the relative importance of urban wealth at periods when it would be most interesting to do so, it so happens, nevertheless, that the exigencies of royal finance have left comprehensive records of two later attempts by the king to conscript the secular wealth of the country. From these it is possible that significant trends may emerge.

The earlier of these attempts was made in 1334 when the king ordered an entirely fresh assessment of the taxes levied on moveable property. Towns and Ancient Demesne were charged at the rate of a tenth, and the rest of the countryside at the rate of a fifteenth of their assessed worth. As on earlier occasions, conventional allowances were made for the things without which a man could not pursue his trade or profession, or maintain his appointed position in the world. There was an exempt minimum; and there were exempt classes and exempt persons—amongst others, the king and his family, the Palatinates, the men of the Cinque Ports, and the men of the Stannaries. These apart, however, few escaped the Commissioners' inquisitorial probe.[12]

The later attempt was made in 1524 as the result of an entirely new tax introduced in the previous year. This tax was graduated somewhat differently from the one levied in 1334, wealth not location being the determining factor; and the rate was lower: the richest paid a twentieth and the poorest less than a fiftieth of their assessed worth. Furthermore land and houses were charged, as well as moveable property, though no one paid on both; and those of sixteen and over who had nothing but wages of not less than £1 per year, paid on them.[13]

[12]J. F. Willard: *Parliamentary Taxes on Personal Property, 1290-1334*, Cambridge, Mass., 1934. Clerical wealth was separately taxed both then and later, the 1524 lay tax being preceded by a huge clerical grant on traditional lines. See F. C. Dietz; English Government Finance, 1485-1558, Illinois, 1920, p. 94.

[13]*Suffolk in 1524*, ed. S. H. A. Hervey, Suffolk Green Books No. 10, Woodbridge, 1910. Introduction, *passim*.

Taxation records are notoriously treacherous documents to interpret, the frailties of assessors and collectors and the subterfuges resorted to by taxpayers being so numerous and varied that a mere recital of the temptations to which taxation infallibly exposes all concerned would quickly lengthen into a catalogue of weakness and venality comprehensive enough to confound all hope of making any practical use of such records whatsoever. For present purposes, however, the shortcomings of tax administration are not to the point, since vigour and laxity, corruption and probity, were probably no more pervasive under one strong king than under another.

Nor is the fact that the taxes of 1334 and 1524 are obviously incommensurable, in itself, a fatal objection to their use; for the comparison to be made is not between 1334 and 1524, but between town and country in 1334 and town and country in 1524.[14]

This does not mean that fundamental changes in the incidence of taxation can be ignored with impunity. By exaggerating the share of urban wealth at one moment, and the share of rural wealth at the next, these taxes could easily make nonsense of all attempts to estimate the relative importance of urban wealth at different periods.

Fortunately for the comparison, what the assessments in fact seem to do is to emphasize the urban element in 1334, when the Commissioners had every official inducement to designate places as towns rather than as villages, so as to make them liable to the higher rate of tax; and to emphasize the rural element in 1524 when taxes on land and wages were added to a revised levy on moveables.

The new tax on wages may not seem, at first sight, to have had this effect. But by 1524 villeinage had virtually disappeared; and farmers who employed men were obliged to pay them wages. Hence with the overwhelming bulk of the population living in the countryside, a tax on wages

[14]Country means county, an arbitrary division imposed by the records but at least the same at both periods.

was, at that period, more likely to have meant a tax on rural wealth than on urban.[15]

Despite this weight of bias towards rural wealth, however, the records make it transparently clear that urban wealth constituted a far larger proportion of total lay wealth in 1524 than it did in 1334. The accompanying Table is unmistakeable upon this point.[16] In county after county the relative importance of urban wealth had risen, often very greatly, by 1524. It was very much the exception for there to have been little or no rise by then.

There is no scholastic legerdemain about this result: on both occasions assessments were made after harvest; neither 1334 nor 1524 seems to have been a year which was unrepresentative of its period[17]; and if the records testify to a relative growth of urban wealth by 1524, that is not simply because of a tendentious reclassification of the places included in the urban category at one time or another. For purposes of analysis only places classified as towns in 1334 were again classified as towns in 1524.

This has not meant accepting meekly the 1334 Commissioners' sometimes extravagant notions of what was town rather than village. Some of the very small places the Commissioners called towns, particularly in the south-western counties, have been struck from the urban side and added to the rural.[18] But it has meant doing flagrant injustice to such places as Westminster, Lavenham, Hadleigh, Enfield, and Henley, which, though they were wealthy towns by 1524, have been counted as villages at both periods because they were assessed as villages in 1334 when

[15] By 1524 labour was cheaper, in real terms, than it had been for a century. Farmers were much more likely therefore to have employed help by then than they had been for a very long time: Seven Centuries, as above.

[16] See Appendix II.

[17] For the wool exports of the 1330's, see above, p. 32; for the cloth exports of the 1520's, see M.M.V., the graph facing p. xviii. For real wages, which were low at both periods, see Seven Centuries.

[18] For the innumerable small towns of medieval Devon, see W. G. Hoskins: The Wealth of Medieval Devon, in *Devonshire Studies*, ed. W. G. Hoskins and H. P. R. Finberg. Jonathan Cape, 1952.

the visiting Commissioners could hardly claim that they were anything else.

Lingering suspicions that this seemingly irrepressible burgeoning of town life is somehow a figment of the records, or a contrivance, may possibly be dispelled by a comparison of certain aspects of the taxation evidence with the independent findings of local history.

We know from Sir Francis Hill's work, for example, that Lincoln stagnated in the later Middle Ages, and from the customs records that Boston utterly lost its commanding position in foreign trade once wool had ceased to be England's chief export. Not the least fascinating of Tout's excursions beyond the frontiers of administrative history was his survey of the stupendous growth of Westminster in the course of the fourteenth century.[19] Yarmouth's problems, officially recognized by 1446, when the town was wholly exempted from the moveables tax, are familiar to readers of Mr Salzman's history of English trade.[20] Southampton's sluggishness in the later Middle Ages, for all its opportunities as the centre of Italian activities in England, has been skilfully elucidated by Miss Coleman from the statistics of its foreign and overland trade.[21] And Coventry's development after 1345, when it got its charter, the resonant theme of Miss Dormer Harris's well-known study, is further illuminated by the aulnage accounts with their revelation of the town's pre-eminence in clothmaking at the end of the fourteenth century, and by the Mayor's census of 1520, which suggests a continuing prosperity by indicating that Coventry had about as many inhabitants then as in 1377, on the eve of the big expansion in clothmaking, when the Poll Tax Commissioners made their reckoning.[22]

[19] T. F. Tout: *Collected Papers*, Manchester, 1934, Vol. III, pp. 249-75.
[20] For the exemptions see Rot. Parl., Vol. V, pp. 6-7, 142, 143-4, 228, 236, etc.; L. F. Salzman: *English Trade in the Middle Ages*, Oxford, 1931.
[21] O. Coleman: in a forthcoming number of *Ec.H.R.*
[22] The Poll Tax put the lay population of 14 and over at 4,817; the Mayor estimated the total population at 6,601: *The Coventry Leet Book*, ed. M. D. Harris, E.E.T.S., Original Series, Vol. 138 (1909), p. 675. For the aulnage records, see above, p. 35.

So radically did the basis of assessment in 1524 differ from the basis of 1334, that any attempt to substantiate the testimony of these historians by comparing urban payments in 1334 with subsequent payments in 1524 and drawing conclusions about urban growth or decline from changes in their size, would constitute an indefensible misuse of evidence. But a comparison of the ratios of the earlier sums paid to the later is not in the least objectionable on such grounds. The ratio in which a single town paid these taxes is, in itself, a meaningless relationship. The disparities that emerge, however, when the ratios in which many towns paid them are compared, seem to bear out what the local historians have discovered, and therefore, may very well tell a good deal about relative rates of urban growth.

Most towns paid their 1334 and 1524 contributions within the range of the ratios 1 : 1 to 1 : 8. At one extreme, Boston which was ruined by the collapse of the foreign trade in wool, has what should properly be called a negative ratio of 2 : 1; at the other, Westminster has the astounding ratio of 1 : 43. Between these extremes were Lincoln and Yarmouth, both paying in the ratio of 1 : 1, which is very low in the range; Southampton, paying in the ratio of 1 : 2, which though it reflects no proud record of growth exactly hits off the distinction between sluggishness and stagnation; and Coventry, paying in the ratio of 1 : 6 which implies notable achievements.[23]

Amongst other towns, the highest rates of growth were achieved by new clothmaking towns such as Lavenham, Colchester, and Exeter; by towns along the main lines of communication such as Dorchester, Henley, and Enfield; and by towns like Reading, which was at once a junction of road and river transport, and, to judge by the rising receipts of its wool and yarn beams, increasingly important industrially.[24]

[23] See Appendix III. Westminster's astonishing growth does not seem to have been in the least an illusion of the records due to special treatment in 1334. See Willard (op. cit., p. 77, note 12), pp. 107, 176.
[24] Reading Corporation Records: Chamberlain's Accounts, passim.

But the fact that urban wealth comprised a far greater proportion of total wealth in 1524 than in 1334, and that some towns grew wealthy more rapidly than others, does not necessarily mean that development was continuous in the period between 1334 and 1524. The decisive change in Reading's wool and yarn beam receipts, which came in the last decade or so of the fifteenth century, serves as a warning against the enticing assumption of a steadily ascending curve of growth.

Nevertheless the changes discussed in previous pages—the prosperity of the later medieval export trade, based on cloth instead of on wool; the extraordinary record of tin output; the constitutional reforms in the towns; the striking rise in the proportion of burgesses to other classes of town-dwellers—all these things point to a fundamental buoyancy and resilience in the town-life of the later Middle Ages that preclude rapid growth in the closing years of the period as a sufficient explanation of the trends revealed in the taxation records.

There is perhaps one final consideration. If growth had indeed occurred solely, or chiefly, in these concluding decades, as a result of the sudden quickening of commercial and industrial opportunities, the burgess rolls, despite their shortcomings, would surely have reflected it. With entry to the burgess ranks as easy, comparatively speaking, as it then was, there would have been a sudden thronging of recruits, such as there was immediately after the Black Death. But there was no such thing. Once the losses of the Black Death had been made good, burgess ranks, on the whole, were recruited at a remarkably steady rate throughout the period that ends with the tax of 1524. There could hardly be a greater tribute to the prosperity of the towns, and hence of the countryside, in the later Middle Ages.

CHAPTER VI

Changes in human affairs rarely bring benefit to all. Political reform must curtail privilege in order to increase equality between persons or classes. Social and economic reform almost invariably sacrifices the interests and property of more fortunate classes to the redress of injuries and injustices done to less fortunate ones. It need not always do so. Far less can be done to relieve poverty, for example, by sharing out the wealth of the rich, than by expediting the economic growth of the community as a whole. Yet even when the relief of poverty has been incidental to a general improvement in the material conditions of life, and has therefore cost the rich nothing, it never fails to provoke from those who sense that there has been a lessening of the distance between the classes, loud complaints of the disrespectful familiarity, unblushing presumption, and flaunting vulgarity, of groups which no longer know their place.

In the thirteenth century, with land-hunger intensifying from decade to decade, it is not difficult to make out at whose expense the achievements of the period were won. The harsh exploitation of villeinage, to which reference has already been made,[1] was matched by real wage-rates which had fallen so low that large employers of labour may very well have taken to heart Walter of Henley's rooted objection to villeins on account of their incorrigible shiftlessness, exchanged villein-labour for wage-labour, and thankfully relied for the quality of the work done on that redoubtable sanction when jobs are few—the threat of the sack.[2]

And what large employers of labour may have done is no more than a very rough guide to the plight of substantial

[1] See above, p. 54, note 5; p. 72, note 4.
[2] Seven Centuries, as above; see also p. 72, note 4. E. Lamond (ed.), *Walter of Henley*, Longmans Green, 1890, p. 11. E. Miller: *The Abbey and Bishopric of Ely*, Cambridge, 1951, p. 103.

numbers, if not of the majority of the population. The history of medieval agriculture depends so largely upon documents which record tenures and their obligations that it is easy to forget the plight of the younger brothers of the tenants whom we meet in these documents, and of the younger sons and younger grandsons, whose prospects of inheriting anything but the family characteristics of their forebears shrank to nothing as population pressure mounted and land ran short. The course of wage-rates, and in particular of real wage-rates, tells us something of their intense distress. But it is unlikely to give us the measure of that distress, not only because money wage-rates tend to lag behind changes in employment opportunities, but also because it is taking much for granted to assume that the large employers from whose records these wage-rates are drawn usually paid the market rate for their labour rather than a conventional rate which they were slow to revise.[3] Occasionally, however, patient quarrying is rewarded and documents come to light which enable us to see things more nearly, perhaps, as they really were. The chance survival of three census returns for a single district in the Fenland[4]; the singularity of a succession of tax collectors in the Hundred of Taunton who returned to the court of the Hundred the fluctuating annual yield of a due owed by all male inhabitants aged twelve and over, instead of compounding for their liabilities by returning the same fixed sum year after year[5]; to accidents and idiosyncrasies such as these we owe horrifying glimpses of a thirteenth-century countryside choked with people. And who can say that even in these glimpses the depths have been plumbed?

In the later Middle Ages, loss of population, by requiting the land-hunger of the survivors of the Black Death, undoubtedly improved out of all recognition the lot of the

[3] E. H. Phelps-Brown and Sheila V. Hopkins: Seven Centuries of Building Wages. *Economica*, August, 1955, pp. 201-2.

[4] H. E. Hallam: Some Thirteenth-Century Censuses. *Ec.H.R.*, Second Series, Vol. X, No. 3 (1958), pp. 340-61.

[5] J. Titow, *op. cit.*, p. 72, note 4, above.

mass of the inhabitants of England. But it would be wrong to represent the period as one of universal emancipation and unqualified gain. Even if it were possible to ignore the tragic loss of life and the transitional disorders provoked by resistance to change, there still remains an irreduceable group of persons, for the most part members of the landed classes, who were outstandingly the casualties of the movements of those momentous times.

Much has been made of the misfortunes of the landed classes in the later Middle Ages. Much also has been made of their immense prosperity, their progressiveness and efficiency, their 'high farming' in the thirteenth century. Yet the assumption that lies behind this rapturous enthusiasm for their achievements and this morbid compassion for their tribulations, the highly questionable assumption that when they flourished the whole world prospered, and when they suffered the whole world was plunged in gloom and depression, is surely the doctrine of *'quand le roi avait bu, la Pologne était ivre'* carried to egregious lengths.

The temptation to be impressed by what is big and successful, or big and sensationally a failure, may be natural enough. But it is an obstacle to the quest for a way of setting the gains of social change against its inescapable losses, and more particularly, for a way of differentiating between changes which inaugurated a period of balanced and fruitful growth, and changes which, seen in a longer perspective, were more akin to a cancerous degeneration of social tissue.

In the thirteenth century the landed classes may have had things very much their own way. But it is exceedingly doubtful whether historians have raised their tremendous edifice of adulation to the thirteenth-century achievements of these classes upon foundations which are anything but exiguous. Achievements there undoubtedly were: managerial reforms; huge investments of capital; improved techniques. These, however, were the achievements of an age when population pressure had severely distorted the structure of society by taking the purchasing power out of wages and profits and handing it over to the landed classes; and when population growth, gathering ever greater momentum, threatened the country with a demographic crisis of stupendous proportions to which there could be only one terrible sequel.

In such circumstances, the fact that they made profits is no proof that the big landlords were efficient farmers. They made profits when it was exceedingly difficult to make losses; when, indeed, they could retrieve all but the most outrageous blunders, more or less painlessly, simply by waiting for rising prices and rents to expunge their errors of judgment.

The ordinary competitive tests of competence cannot be applied to their activities. They ran no risk of being dispossessed in favour of more energetic and enterprising farmers who could offer the king higher rents than they could afford to pay. Such was the nature of feudal tenure that it utterly precluded anything so straightforwardly commercial as a take-over bid in the modern manner.[6] And although some of them improved their estates in spectacular ways, since we cannot compare their returns on these improvements with the returns that the resources they employed might have procured elsewhere, we cannot be at all confident that the big thirteenth-century landlords used these resources anything like as frugally as they, or others, might have done.

They all instituted a great deal of paper-work: manorial extents—in effect estimates of expected yields—were prepared, and annual accounts were returned according to standardized models and a widely recognized procedure. But to a generation bemused by bureaucracy it is not self-evident that flourishing office work is a guarantee of good farming.

There was nothing, for example, to prevent landlords from revising their extents so as to increase the obligations

[6]For the reliefs paid, see I. J. Saunders: *Feudal Military Service in England*, Oxford, 1956, Appendix I; S. Painter: *Studies in the History of the English Feudal Barony*, Baltimore, 1943, pp. 63-4.

for which their manors were liable. Indeed without some such revision improving landlords could scarcely hope to benefit by the greater productivity their reforms were intended to achieve. And from time to time, on certain estates, the extents actually were revised, as vigour supplanted lethargy at the top, or as hard times, over-spending, the charges upon alienation and succession, escheats, forfeitures, wardships, and marriages, left burdens which only desperate measures could relieve.

Extents are not as numerous as they might be. And historians have not, on the whole, given to the notion of economic efficiency the attention they have given to the impressive splendour of the things certain big thirteenth-century landlords did with their estates. But from what little they say, and from personal impressions, it would seem that revision of their extents was very far from being the rule with thirteenth-century landlords. Walter of Henley, leading contemporary writer though he may have been, while he exhorted his readers to have extents prepared, said nothing whatsoever about the need to safeguard subsequent achievements in productivity by subsequent amendment of these extents. In his opinion, indeed, the main purpose of extents was not an ambitious one: it was to circumscribe idleness and corruption by acting as a check upon what was returned in the annual accounts.[7] And since these accounts, though carefully drafted and punctiliously examined, were chiefly records of the discharge of obligations laid down in the extents, the big landlords were

---

[7] N. Denholm-Young: *Seigneurial Administration in England*, Oxford, 1937, pp. 128-30; D. Oschinsky: Medieval Treatises on Estate Accounting, *Ec.H.R.*, Vol. 17 (1947), pp. 52-61; J. S. Drew: The Manorial Accounts of St Swithun's Priory, Winchester, *E.H.R.*, Vol. 62 (1947), p. 25. Medieval bailiffs had a reputation for oppressing the tenantry; see, for example, T. F. T. Plucknett: *The Medieval Bailiff*, The Creighton Lecture, 1952, Athlone Press, 1954. To the extent that they deserved it, the deficiencies of the demesne system were at any rate partially offset: the bailiff acting as a sort of tenant-farmer was getting more from the land than his lord received. See J. S. Drew (*op. cit.*, pp. 39-40) for some suggestions that yields may sometimes have been greater than they appeared to be.

caught in a web of usage from which it required exceptional courage and imagination to escape, and were irresistibly tempted to accept what had been done in the past as the surest guide to what ought to be done in the future.

In normal circumstances, therefore, the extent was less likely to have been a spur to effort and hence a register of feudal burdens multiplied and customary obligations redoubled, than an excuse for inertia and a refuge for laxity.

Everything in fact conspired to shield the big landlord from having to respond fully to the clamorous opportunities of the age—a tenurial system which gave him resources for which he did not pay the market price; population pressure which kept agricultural prices high; an accounting system which provided a test of solvency rather than a test of profitability; and, it should be added, a system of husbandry in many of the most populous shires that scattered the demesne strips amongst the rest in the open fields and thus made close control of farming techniques impossible.

Is it any wonder that the lords of those huge, unwieldy, and often scattered estates of small farms, about which modern historians write so admiringly, rarely achieved the cereal yields regarded as reasonable by the authors of the farming manuals they cherished, and copied, and handed down from generation to generation?[8]

Moreover, if the big landlords who commonly held the bulk of their possessions for life as tenants-in-chief of the king had little inducement to be anything but wasteful and inefficient farmers, lesser men, in so far as their holdings

[8] R. V. Lennard: The Alleged Exhaustion of the Soil in Medieval England, *Ec. Journal*, Vol. 32 (1922), pp. 19-20; M. K. Bennet: British Wheat Yields Per Acre for Seven Centuries, *Ec. History*, Vol. 3, No. 10 (1935), *passim*; H. W. Saunders (ed.): *An Introduction to the Obedientiary Rolls of Norwich Cathedral Priory*, Norwich, 1930, pp. 12, 48, *et seq.*; J. S. Drew *op. cit.*, above, p. 87, note 7), p. 32; J. A. Raftis: *The Estates of Ramsay Abbey*, Toronto, 1957, pp. 174-8; R. A. L. Smith: *Canterbury Cathedral Priory*, Cambridge, 1943, p. 135. The Canterbury case is particularly interesting, for Canterbury kept an unusually large collection of treatises: E. Lamond (as above, p. 83, note 2), pp. xl, and 71; also, D. Oschinsky: Medieval Treatises on Estate Management, *Ec.H.R.*, Second Series, Vol. 8, No. 3 (1956), pp. 298-9.

were not for life, had every inducement to farm without thought for the future. For the law recognized no principle of compensation for improvements; and as rents rose, landlords who shortened leases and imposed tenancies-at-will, though they made certain that rising land values would enrich them rather than their tenants, made inevitable some deterioration of long-term productivity.[9]

In some ways, conditions in thirteenth-century England, despite immense differences in social and political circumstances, had affinities with conditions in Ireland before the Great Famine. In both countries population pressure increasingly governed economic change; in both, the landlords, generally speaking, had every excuse to respond sluggishly, if at all, to the challenging opportunities of their times. There was the same rapid dissolution of holdings as the peasants multiplied; the same insecurity of tenure; the same heedlessness of the future.[10]

'With a population pressing against the means of subsistence,' said Ricardo, 'the only remedies are either a reduction of people or a more rapid accumulation of capital.'[11] In medieval England, as in nineteenth-century Ireland, it was left to famine and pestilence to lift the burden of overpopulation. And when that burden had been lifted there was, in both countries, the same extraordinary transformation of the living conditions of the mass of the people.

In England this transformation was accompanied by what was probably a vast improvement in the standards of husbandry that ordinary farmers observed. It may seem paradoxical to argue that standards of husbandry improved in a period when cheap land and dear labour were forcing

[9] E. Miller (op. cit., p. 83, note 2, above), pp. 109-11; F. L. Ganshof: Medieval Agrarian Society in its Prime, Camb. Ec. Hist. of Europe, Vol. I, ed. J. H. Clapham and E. Power, Cambridge, 1942, p. 309.

[10] For some remarkable evidence of the dissolution of holdings, see M. Postan and C. N. L. Brooke (eds.), The Carte Nativorum, Northamptonshire Record Society, Vol. 20, 1960, passim. On Ireland, see above, p. 53, note 3.

[11] On the Principles of Political Economy and Taxation. The Works and Correspondence of David Ricardo. Ed. P. Sraffa, Vol. I, Cambridge, 1951, p. 99.

landlords to abandon arable farming. But landlords, if they may be judged by their thirteenth-century record, had made indifferent farmers; it is unlikely therefore that their going was a loss to agriculture. Moreover there is a far more important consideration. In England, as in Ireland, the greater part of the land had never been farmed by landlord and bailiff. It had always been farmed by the peasantry.[12] And the effect of relief from population pressure was to make the peasantry not more heedless of the future but infinitely less so.

In this connexion there are fascinating similarities between England in the later Middle Ages and Ireland in the later nineteenth century. The law did not concern itself in England, as it did in Ireland after 1870, with the compensation of tenants for improvements which they had made to their landlords' property. But as land became more abundant, in the course of the fourteenth century, landlords were obliged to lengthen leases as well as to lower rents; and leases seem to have got so much longer than the useful life of the most enduring improvements that ordinary medieval farmers could afford to make that they effectually nullified the evil consequences of the law's shortcomings.

What is most striking, however, and indeed illuminating, about any comparison between England and Ireland in the period following their respective years on the anvil, is not the experiences they shared; it is the astounding contrasts to be found in their response to the incalculable possibilities of a new age. The comparison is not, perhaps, altogether fair, since Protestant landlordism and the avalanche of cheap foodstuffs from oversea set problems for nineteenth-century Ireland such as later medieval England, with its incomparable natural resources and compact and relatively tranquil social system, never had to solve. Nevertheless it is not wholly inadmissible; for it is impossible to believe that Irish stagnation is predominantly the fault of

[12] See, for example, the discussion in W. J Ashley: *The Bread of Our Forefathers*, Oxford, 1928, p. 86.

the English when one reflects that, after forty years as a republic, Ireland is still a country whose economic stability depends partly upon emigration and remittances from abroad.

Unlike Ireland, which by the standards of such contemporaries as Denmark, changed very slowly in the half-century following the Great Famine, England responded to the demographic catastrophes of the fourteenth century with a release of energy and enterprise so prodigious as to make it something of a cynosure of foreign eyes. It is with this response that previous chapters have been chiefly concerned.

For the survivors, the fourteenth-century famines and pestilences were, no doubt, on personal grounds, inexpressibly grievous. But they unlocked a cornucopia. England was given a sort of Marshall Aid on a stupendous scale. To put the thing another way, the moving frontier was restored without the stringencies that commonly go with heroic times. Land was not merely abundant; it was equipped, and stocked, and often, perhaps, enriched rather than impoverished by the husbandry of generations of peasants.[13]

Such gains were not necessarily permanent. Land, stock, and equipment, all had to be maintained and replaced. And in an age of rising wage-rates, costs of repair and renewal might very well be thought to have discouraged the farmers since it was they who were presumably compelled to incur them. Farming landlords were unquestionably discouraged by the rise of these costs as they were by the rise of other labour costs. But rising wage-rates did not discourage the peasants. And if they did not do so that was surely because the sudden superfluity of things gave the peasants something more than material means. It gave them an opportunity to work such as few had enjoyed in the days when resources of land and capital were scarce and labourers idle

[13] Land which had been in demesne was usually well-manured, if only because of the lord's right to fold his tenants' animals on his own land.

because they were relatively too numerous. And in the end, as the landlords withdrew altogether from farming, the peasants, fortified by ample tenancies and long leases, entered into their own. The low cereal prices of the later Middle Ages call to mind Arthur Young's comment upon the French peasantry, that 'the magic of property turns sand into gold'. They bear witness to the tireless industry of countless peasant families which had little use for hired labour, and none for managerial expenses, either in the running or in the general maintenance of their farms.

*   *   *

By enriching the peasantry in this fashion, not for the hour, but for several generations, the pestilences established a new structure of prices which had consequences of the utmost importance for the whole community.

We know all too little about the prices of agricultural products other than cereals. Thorold Rogers concluded, from what he could find, that they changed very little, if at all, in the later Middle Ages.[14] But even if many had fallen, as cereal prices had done, so sharply did wage-rates rise that manufactures probably rose in price, more or less in proportion to the amount of labour that went to their making; and services, consummate examples of labour-intensive commodities, probably rose highest of all.[15]

This meant a massive diversion of resources, not only from those whose incomes from land were smaller than before, but even from those whose incomes from land, though perhaps nominally unchanged, or it may be, somewhat increased, in fact bought fewer manufactured goods and services than hitherto.

Ecclesiastical acquisition of land, for example, virtually ceased in the later Middle Ages, with the result that ecclesiastical revenues, unless recruited by efficient manage-

[14] *Work and Wages*, p. 237.

[15] With differentials narrowing, skill made less difference than it might have done: see above, p. 63. For the rise in the wages of mercenaries, see, for example, H. J. Hewitt: *The Black Prince's Expedition of 1355-7*, Manchester, 1958.

ment, fell disastrously in money terms, and hence even more disastrously in real value.[16]

Influential and resourceful lay families of all degrees could usually retrieve wasted fortunes, or enhance their wealth and power, by means of prudent marriage, inheritance, litigation, and preferment. In the thirteenth century they could generally restore or improve their standing at the expense of the peasantry. Only a very few ever made fortunes by farming land acquired and held on commercial terms. Petty's dictum that 'there is much more to be gained by manufacture than husbandry, and by merchandize than manufacture'[17] is far more than a cheerless reflexion upon the treacherous climate and endless soil variations of England: it is a sober recognition of the hostages that farming gives to fortune in the shape of a prolonged investment cycle, heavy overhead charges, and an output which is almost unalterable once decisions about crops have been put in hand.

In the later Middle Ages such families could no longer hope to maintain the purchasing power of their incomes by battening on the peasantry. They could not yet do so by despoiling the Church, though there was a moment, in the late fourteenth century, when Parliament got very close to anticipating the Reformation. And if they could still marry, and inherit, and go to law, and seek lucrative perquisites from the king, they gained thereby, not as a class, but for the most part, at one another's expense.

With times against them the best they could do was to circumscribe their losses. To some extent they could do this, and more, by prudent investment of the spoils of a war with France which was always fought on foreign soil, and which, as Mr McFarlane has suggested, could usually be made to pay.[18] To some extent they were able to exploit

[16] The fact that the later Middle Ages was a great period of chantry-founding does not make very much difference to the argument.

[17] *The Economic Writings of Sir William Petty*, ed. C. H. Hull, Cambridge, 1899, Vol. I, p. 256.

[18] The Investment of Sir John Fastolf's Profits of War, *Trans. R.H.S.*, Fifth Series, Vol. 7, 1957, *passim*.

the recurrent weaknesses of later medieval kings who, until Edward IV's time, squandered in their favour an inheritance of landed wealth greater, after Henry IV's accession, than any that preceding kings had enjoyed.[19] But their chief defence against the erosion of the resources of their class lay in Parliament, which steadfastly refused indiscriminate supply to kings as unsuccessful militarily and as prodigal financially as Richard II and all but one of the Lancastrians proved to be.

If Parliament became increasingly grudging over supply, that was not, as is often said, because the country was too poor for it to be anything else. For one thing, English standards of poverty, when it comes to taxation, have always been extremely high. The absence of land frontiers with powerful adversaries has always made it difficult for English governments to carry conviction with a plea of *raison d'état*; so that the reluctance of later medieval Parliaments to finance their kings is much more likely to reflect their disillusionment with them than to reflect anything else. For another thing, the shift of economic forces that enriched the peasantry prevented those who granted these Parliamentary taxes from passing their burden on. As land ceased to command a premium, the taxes levied in the countryside, where the main contribution was made, were absorbed, perforce, by the landed classes which received the low rents of the period; they were no longer paid, as in effect they had been in the past, by tenants compelled to enter into agreements upon their landlords' terms.

Later medieval governments were quick to grasp the implications of this change, and at intervals throughout the fifteenth century introduced experimental taxes, usually on a pound-rate basis instead of on the customary basis of county quotas, which were devised to penetrate traditional appearances and get at the real wealth of the

[19] B. P. Wolffe: Acts of Resumption in the Lancastrian Parliaments, 1399-1456, E.H.R., Vol. 73 (1958), pp. 583-613.

country.[20] On the whole these experiments failed; and the landed classes, since they continued to bear a heavier burden of taxation than in the past, got keener than they had ever been on value for money.

Nor was this the only shift of economic forces to strengthen later medieval Parliaments in vehement and unmanageable ways, and enable them to be plain-spoken on occasions to the point of fomenting sedition. There was also the decline of the wool export trade; a decline which meant not only that foreign consumers subscribed less and less lavishly than before, through the payment of wool duties, to the cost of England's wars, but also that such revenues as the Crown could enjoy virtually without reference to Parliament, were disconcertingly curtailed at a period which was, for it, one of great financial stringency.

Not that Parliament always carried parsimony to the point of miserliness. There were occasions when the right man came forward to do the popular thing and convinced Parliament that he could succeed. Such a man was Henry V. And until his debts overwhelmed him, Parliament granted supply in the traditional manner with unmeasured liberality.

With a population very much smaller than it had been in the days of Crécy and Poitiers, it might be supposed that the burden of grants of supply which were comparable with the ones made then would weigh intolerably upon all classes. But even when Parliament was at its most magnanimous, owing to the great change in the structure of prices that had taken place since the mid-fourteenth century, its grants, in so far as they were spent on other things than food, gave Henry V command of many fewer resources than similar grants had given to Edward III. War therefore, even at its most demanding, was unlikely to have absorbed more of the *per capita* wealth of the community in the fifteenth century than it had done in the fourteenth.

[20] For a convenient summary of these, see F. C. Dietz (*op. cit.*, above, p. 77, note 12), pp. 11-18; also, W. R. Ward: *The English Land Tax in the Eighteenth Century*, Oxford, 1953, for some interesting remarks on pound-rate taxes and county quotas.

And it was not often in the later Middle Ages that Parliament allowed war to be so demanding. Occasions when Parliamentary confidence in the king and his Council was not misplaced and betrayed were few. The dreary record of misappropriated supply and failure to redeem alienated royal revenue made Parliament intensely critical and wary.[21] It also drove it more than once to intervene, on behalf of the taxpayer, in the government of the country.

Parliament was very well informed, particularly in the fifteenth century, as to the state of the Exchequer.[22] And by 1433, when things had got so bad that a new Treasurer was obliged to institute an elaborate and expensive investigation of the Crown's financial position,[23] Parliament resorted to a further measure of control: it cut by 10·4 per cent the value of a grant of moveables which had stood unchanged since 1334 at a conventional figure of about £38,000.[24]

If this is yet another symptom of the progressive impoverishment of later medieval England, then it is certainly a very curious one. For the remissions of 1433 were followed two years later by a fairly successful experimental income tax which yielded twice as much as they had excused.[25] Moreover, the remissions themselves are inherently suspect. If they were really granted because the country could bear the burden of a full grant no longer, then it is surely odd that relief was so rarely given to those in greatest need. Every county got a remission of 10·4 per cent of its quota,

[21] Wolffe, op. cit., passim.

[22] Wolffe, op. cit., p. 594, and note 1. Before 1433 Exchequer assessments of revenue and expenditure were prepared, strictly speaking, for the exclusive benefit of king and Council. But wind of them was bound to have spread to leading Parliamentarians, if not to the rank and file.

[23] J. L. Kirby: The Issues of the Lancastrian Exchequer and Lord Cromwell's Estimates of 1433. Bulletin of the Institute of Historical Research, Vol. 24, No. 70, 1951, pp. 121-51. Mr Kirby believes that Cromwell exaggerated the extent of the crisis of 1433. He may very well be right. But the point here is that Parliament had no reason to go behind a full Exchequer inquiry; and in view of the failure of policies of resumption, reacted vigorously when that inquiry seemed to justify its worst fears.

[24] Rot. Parl., IV, p. 425.

[25] H. L. Gray: Incomes from Land in England in 1436, E.H.R., Vol. 49 (1934), p. 612.

as if all were equally poor.[26] And within the counties local authorities seem to have been no less indifferent to special circumstances than the government had been. In some counties, such as Essex, every village got a straight 10·4 per cent remission of its usual contribution[27]; in others, such as Norfolk and Devon, the distribution of relief had little or no bearing upon the comparative wealth or poverty of particular regions[28]; and elsewhere, as in Wiltshire, the mark of influence and patronage is sometimes to be found decisively stamped upon the records. The city of Salisbury, for example, was awarded a very much greater remission when its overlord, the Bishop, was on the Commission than when he was not.[29]

*   *   *

The cut of 10·4 per cent that Parliament imposed in 1433, it increased to 15 per cent in 1446, at a time when government debt had swollen monstrously.[30] From one point of view this astonishing stand by Parliament in 1433 and 1446 could be regarded as yet another demonstration, albeit a momentous one, of the moral and financial bankruptcy of the Crown, and of the penury, obstinacy, and faithlessness, of the landed classes. But there was surely another element in the situation, one which was a result of the profound effect of the new balance of wealth upon the social and political structure of the country. This was the influence exerted by middle classes which had been enriched by the burgess prosperity to which a good deal of this essay has been devoted; sometimes perhaps at the expense of a profligate Crown; and not least by the transfer from them to the landed classes of that part of the true burden of the moveables taxes that the landed classes had

[26] P.R.O. E.371/199, *passim*. I am indebted to Miss O. Coleman for this information.

[27] P.R.O. E.179 *s.v.* Essex.

[28] *Norfolk Archaeology*, Vol. 12 (1895), p. 258; W. G. Hoskins: The Wealth of Medieval Devon, in W. G. Hoskins and H. P. R. Finberg: *Devonshire Studies*, Jonathan Cape, 1952, p. 249. The Cambridgeshire Brecklands are another example of an impoverished area getting no special relief: P.R.O. E.179/81/80, etc.

[29] P.R.O. E.371/199, E.179/196/99A.

[30] *Rot. Parl.* V, pp. 6-9.

once been able to pass on to them, either directly in higher food and raw material prices, or indirectly by way of higher rents for the land upon which food and raw materials were grown. Their influence may very well have been substantial, at times even, decisive. Without reckoning with it, indeed, one can scarcely hope to understand the significance of the immense change that took place, during the later Middle Ages, in the importance of Parliament in government and of the Commons in Parliament. In the states of medieval Germany, as Professor Carsten has brilliantly argued, the social compactness of the trading and landed classes was of enormous value in fortifying the various Parliaments in their dealings with their respective dukes.[31] In England the increasing wealth of the burgess class enabled leading merchants to arrogate to themselves the style and dignity of such titles as Esquire and Gentleman and thus to meet the Knights of the Shire as much on terms of social equality as of common interest. Nothing is more likely, therefore, than that Parliament's resolution in the teeth of the Crown's demands drew its strength from social developments which were comparable with those that were taking place in contemporary Germany.

It would be a gross anachronism to attribute to Parliament, in the later Middle Ages, anything like the commanding ascendancy in government that actually belonged, as Fortescue clearly perceived, to King and Council. Moreover after the mid-fifteenth century the burgess members of Parliament began an exodus which, in the end, left the Commons with only a tiny group of mercantile representatives until the Reform Parliament met in 1834, and thus rendered nugatory the bonds of interest and social affinity that they had so recently forged with the Knights of the Shire.[32]

[31] F. L. Carsten: *Princes and Parliaments in Germany*, Oxford, 1959.

[32] Professor J. S. Roskell, in his *The Commons in the Parliament of 1422*, p. 51, identified the trading and industrial interests of only forty burgess members. This does not mean that in 1422 there were only forty burgess members who were merchants or manufacturers. See M. McKisack (*op. cit.*, above, p. 19, note 17), pp. 98, 118, etc.; V.C.H. Wilts., Vol. IV, for the Parliamentary history of the county.

The displacement of burgesses, in many urban consti-tuencies, by lawyers and country gentlemen, may have been forced upon some towns by poverty. But Parliament was not the natural arena for merchants that it was, until recently, for their successors. The burgess members left Par-liament, essentially, because their work in Parliament was done. Wool politics lost much of their urgency once the wool export trade had dwindled to an annual trickle. And with the age of charters drawing inevitably to a close, the towns had achieved their chief object in sending members to Parliament, which was, in the words of a Norwich record, 'to increase our liberties as they may be able'.[33] For the rest, there were the insistent and persuasive blandish-ments of local potentates who, as the Earl of Westmorland reminded the burgesses of Grimsby in 1470, by supplying members for urban seats, could promote the interests of the towns without adding to their charges and in so doing enable them to earn the goodwill of powerful neighbours.[34]

Nevertheless royal bankruptcy and Parliamentary solidarity, while they lasted, put an iron curb on monarchi-cal power. The courts, even at the very end of the Middle Ages, denied greater rights to a king than those provided for ordinary citizens by private law.[35] In principle, there-fore, England enjoyed greater freedom from arbitrary government, in the later Middle Ages, than it would enjoy again for over a century. It was a precarious freedom; for it depended very largely upon the insolvency and personal incapacity of the king. And with the accession of Edward IV and the ending of the war with France, the age of impotent, vaccillating, and bankrupt kings came to an end.[36]

Nor was freedom without its cost. Weak kings meant

[33] M. McKisack, op. cit., p. 119.

[34] M. McKisack, op. cit., pp. 62-3.

[35] T. F. T. Plucknett: The Lancastrian Constitution, in Tudor Studies, ed. R. W. Seton-Watson (1924), pp. 161-81.

[36] K. B. McFarlane: Bastard Feudalism, Bulletin of the Institute of Historical Research, Vol. 20, No. 61 (1945), pp. 161-80.

weak government; and when government was weak private armies multiplied, civil disquiet deepened, and undue influence, whether exercised clandestinely by way of patronage, or flagrantly in faction and caucus, gained an unwonted franchise. Pernicious growths such as these, drawing strength from the discomfiture of the central authority, unquestionably made for anxious times in the later Middle Ages.

Anxious times, however, were not new to English public life. Between 1066 and 1377, as Sir Frank Stenton once reminded the Historical Association, there were only two periods when general peace prevailed in England for thirty consecutive years.[37] Peace was often broken without serious consequences; for violence was not invariably widespread or on the grand scale. But no less could be said of the fifteenth century. The Wars of the Roses, indeed, seem to differ from comparably systematic insurrections of earlier times, such as the Barons' War, chiefly in that more of what contemporaries said about them has survived.

Certainly public disorder, in the later Middle Ages, was never great enough to turn England into a paradise of private empires ruled over by implacable grandees. There was no freemasonry between those who gambled for the highest stakes, who lavished upon retainers the revenues they no longer contributed to the financing of foreign war, who wrecked and despoiled, annexed and abducted, perjured themselves and corrupted others. Such men were more often adversaries than confederates, and their clashing ambitions weakened them locally. If the Paston Letters teach one lesson more clearly than another, it is surely, as Mr McFarlane has contended, that these rivals for local suzerainty could not intimidate and terrorize even for such purposes as Parliamentary election. Constituencies had to be nursed and managed. 'Even at the height of a civil war in which the landed classes at least were risking their lives and fortunes, when the country swarmed with armed men

[37] The Changing Feudalism of the Middle Ages, *History*, Vol. 19, No. 76 (1935), pp. 289-301.

fresh from victories in the field of battle and when the Sheriff was a notorious partisan, the winning side could not be sure of returning its own men. Those to whom the electors "gave their voices" were not necessarily the candidates for whom a Duke had "written" . . . Management was already a necessary art for those who wished to influence elections.'[38]

*　　　*　　　*

And Pastons' England was one to which few fifteenth-century Englishmen cared to belong. For the mass of the population the quarrels and intrigues of the opposing factions of Lancaster and York, the private feuds of the nobility, and even the toppling of kings from their thrones, were usually remote and transpontine happenings from which it was glad to remain aloof and to whose issues it was profoundly indifferent.

The invincible unconcern of the citizens of Norwich, a city in the heart of the Paston country, with the strenuous drama of Paston wrangles and dynastic strife that was being enacted all about them, has often been remarked upon.[39] It was not exceptional. Citizens of towns and cities throughout the country, as the records of their corporate activities indicate, were no more concerned than were the citizens of Norwich with the envenomed rivalries that estranged their local county and noble families from one another. Still less were they concerned with nice questions of loyalty to anointed or appointed kings. They changed allegiance with shameless apostasy; shuffled off embarrassing ties without demur or scruple; when in doubt temporized cynically; lent money to both sides, if necessary at the same time; and swore vows of unswerving devotion to whichever usurper happened to be the true king by dint of having the stronger forces in their neighbourhood, or in the country as a whole. Their business was trade and

---

[38] Parliament and Bastard Feudalism, *Trans. R.H.S.*, Fourth Series, Vol. 26 (1944), p. 63.

[39] Thus, *Town Life*, Vol. I, p. 37, note i; W. I. Haward: Economic Aspects of the Wars of the Roses in East Anglia, *E.H.R.*, Vol. 41 (1926), p. 174.

industry, and politics mattered to them only when they thought that local interests were at stake.

This tranquil detachment from the contentions of the age was not confined to the towns. Economic life could never have been as robust as this essay has tried to show that it was, had large sections of the community been actively involved in current seditions and conspiracies. The cloth and tin production figures, in this context, speak for themselves. The low and steady cereal prices indicate how little the disorders of the period affected the farmers. C. L. Kingsford's work upon their family papers testifies to the rustic contentment in which those members of the gentry dwelt whose ambitions did not take them into politics. And two remarkable series of records, the Brokage Books of Southampton and the Rolls of the Court of Common Pleas, enormously strengthen the presumption that England was substantially untroubled by the multiplicity of mischiefs of which Shakespeare and his fellow-idolaters of Tudor despotism made so much. The Southampton toll books are a revelation of the volume of carts which, throughout the fifteenth century, left Southampton by the North Gate and placidly jogged their loads of French wine and Italian woad along ancient trunk roads to places as far away as Coventry and Oxford, as well as to London and to towns nearer home[40]; while the records of the Court of Common Pleas display the calm dignity with which a distinguished court transacted its business with all the counties of England unhampered by the lawlessness and divisions of the age, maintained its personnel virtually intact despite the vicissitudes of fifteenth-century public life, and refined its processes in order to deal with the ever-increasing quantity of litigation that came its way.[41]

*　　　*　　　*

[40] *The Brokage Book of Southampton 1443-4*, Vol. I, ed. O. Coleman, Southampton Record Series, Vol. 4 (1960), Introduction, *passim*.

[41] P.R.O. C.P.40, *passim*; M. Hastings: *The Court of Common Pleas*, Cornell, 1947. Dr Hastings' answer (p. 7) to Holdsworth's charge, for which see above, p. 19, is that cases to support a plea of corruption are to be found at all times.

Undistracted by politics and enriched by a prodigious transfer of control over the resources of the economic system, the middle classes and the peasantry, during the later Middle Ages, entered upon a period of domestic comfort so astonishing by the standards of the time as to rouse passionate expressions of enthusiasm and disgust. It would be easier to write down Fortescue's glowing account of the material well-being of his fellow-countrymen as the work of a sentimental exile idealizing the past, were it not for the corroboration of travelled foreigners such as Froissart and Philip de Commines, and of men with as little sympathy with the social movements of their day as Gower, Lydgate, and Hoccleve. There is, moreover, the concern of Parliament to add weight to their words. The growth of ostentation that a mass of Parliamentary petitions deplored and sumptuary legislation fitfully attempted to restrain, was accompanied, according to statute, by the neglect of arms drill for games, and by a disturbing migration of farm labourers to the towns, where the men lived idly and their children were apprenticed to crafts.[42]

A great deal of the history of the increasing material comfort of the poorer classes, whenever it has occurred, could be written in terms of the scandalized alarm, the haughty disapprobation, and the dark forebodings, expressed by men who felt that society was being threatened by what they denounced as the growing idleness and dissipation of contemporaries, and later and cooler observers usually applauded as a growth of leisure and a broader choice of things to buy and do. Much of the evidence for such increasing comfort in the later Middle Ages is lost, though the prosperity of the towns depended substantially upon catering for it. We know virtually nothing about the housing of yeomen and husbandmen whose rise from bondage was the phenomenon of the age. We know scarcely more about their food, except that it undoubtedly im-

[42] F. E. Baldwin: *Sumptuary Legislation and Personal Regulation in England*, Baltimore, 1926; W. Stubbs: *The Constitutional History of England*, Fourth Edition, Vol. III, p. 621, *et seq.*; *Social England*, pp. 22-3.

proved, or about their drink, though with cereal prices low, it probably included a great deal more ale and beer than it had ever done before.

We do know, however, that per head of the population there was far more tin available than hitherto, and may conclude, therefore, that pewterware was probably commoner in humble homes than it had been formerly.[43] And we also know that as commercial clothmaking grew, the proportion of total output retained internally grew even more rapidly. Of this trend worsteds are an interesting example: for while the export of worsteds declined sharply in the fifteenth century, the number of new burgesses entering the worsted crafts at Norwich, which was the centre of the industry, probably declined but little, if it declined at all.[44]

The market for imported goods was perhaps no less profoundly affected than other markets by the social and industrial changes of the fourteenth century. But the goods imported by native merchants, except for wine, were not taxed at all until 1347, and thereafter were taxed only intermittently until late in the fourteenth century. Hence statistical analysis of the customs records cannot yield comprehensive results to match those of a recent study of the chief exports. The historian is thrown back upon personal impressions. Nevertheless there can be little doubt that the import trade reflected the changes of the time. Salt which had once been, on balance, an export, was being imported, by the late fourteenth century, in far greater volume than it had ever gone abroad, rising labour costs having made the English product largely unsaleable.[45] Can-

[43] It is impossible to be more exact about this because we cannot estimate the export trade in tin until late in the fourteenth century. Even the alien share of the trade, in the earlier period before the population fell, must remain a mystery owing to the loss of the bulk of the particulars of account of the customs levied on alien goods: P.R.O. E.122, passim; D.C.O. Ministers' Accounts, Rolls 1-4.

[44] See above, p. 49, note 28. For worsted exports, see E. M. Carus-Wilson and O. Coleman, as above, p. 27, note 6.

[45] A. R. Bridbury: England and the Salt Trade in the Later Middle Ages, Oxford, 1955.

vas, whose manufacture was by then contributing very greatly to the development of Normandy and Brittany, seems to have found a growing market in England.[46] The later medieval records of cities such as Louvain that tell of a rising output of tapestry and linen goods strengthen the impression conveyed by family papers, inventories, and customs accounts, of an increasing import into England of things that were bought far more rarely in earlier times.[47] Certainly wine consumption per head, at least until the French war entered upon its concluding phase, was as great as it had ever been, despite a tripling of its average retail price.[48]

The higher standards of domestic comfort enjoyed by classes which hitherto had been the drudges and minions of the social system, and the quickening of their social aspirations, reveal themselves in myriad ways. Amongst those who could afford very much more than wattle-and-daub, they reveal themselves in the handsome and spacious houses, with their glazed windows and wings thrown out from a central hall for the sake of privacy from servants and visitors, that took the place of the cramped quarters in which previous generations had lived.[49] They reveal themselves in the books of etiquette devoured by the new middle classes as they struggled with novel and perplexing social difficulties[50]; and in the tremendous educational effort of

[46] M. Mollat: Le Commerce Maritime Normand, Paris, 1952, pp. 166-7.

[47] I am indebted to M. Raymond Van Uytven for this information about Louvain; see also his: La Flandre et le Brabant, 'terres de promission' sous les ducs de Bourgogne?, Revue du Nord, Vol. 43, No. 172 (1961), pp. 281-317.

[48] M. K. James: The Fluctuations of the Anglo-Gascon Wine Trade during the Fourteenth Century, Ec.H.R., Second Series, Vol. IV, No. 2, 1951, pp. 170-96; M.M.V., Chapter VII, passim.

[49] A. Hamilton Thompson: The English House. Historical Association Pamphlet, No. 105 (1936), reprinted in G. Barraclough (ed.): Social Life in Early England, London, 1960. See also, Thos. Wright: A History of Domestic Manners and Sentiments in England, London, 1862.

[50] The Babees Book, ed. F. J. Furnivall, E.E.T.S., Original Series, No. 32 (1868); A Fifteenth Century Courtesy Book, ed. R. W. Chambers, E.E.T.S., Original Series, Vol. 148 (1914).

the later Middle Ages, with its new schools, its new Inns of Court for the training not only of lawyers, but also, as Fortescue reminded his readers, of civil servants and administrators, and its new colleges at Oxford and Cambridge for the pursuit of postgraduate work.[51] They reveal themselves in the conquest of England by the English language; in the birth of a new dramatic form, the Craft Miracle Play, which was essentially a product of the resurgent towns; in the banishment of poetry from Court to inn and market-place, where ballad, and lyric, and carol, enriched the lives of new classes of patrons. And they reveal themselves in the momentous event of the year 1476—the setting up of a printing press at Westminster by Caxton, who as an ex-Governor of the Merchant Adventurers Company was not a man to misconstrue commercial portents.[52]

The emergence of the middle classes as a political force in the later Middle Ages is part of the constitutional history of England. The emergence of small farmers and artisans from the obscurity of the world of village and manor into something like public life was perhaps, in its own way, hardly less remarkable. The records of the Court of Common Pleas abound with evidence of the litigation that homely countrymen brought in growing volume to Westminster from the local courts of the provinces.[53] The thronging of the County Courts with 'people of small substance and no value' presuming to vote at election time 'with the most worthy knights and squires resident' pro-

[51] A. F. Leach: *The Schools of Medieval England*, Methuen, 1915; also his Some Results of Research in the History of Education in England, *Proc. of the British Academy*, Vol. VI (1914), pp. 433-80. Leach's claims for medieval education were often ill-founded and extravagant. But the trend he stressed was plainly important. On the Inns of Court, see *Social England*, p. 91; for the new colleges at Oxford and Cambridge, see above, p. 75, note 10.

[52] *Prejudice and Promise*; H. S. Bennet: *Chaucer and the Fifteenth Century*, Oxford, 1948; E. K. Chambers: *English Literature at the Close of the Middle Ages*, Oxford, 1947.

[53] The bulk of the entries in the Plea Rolls are formal: litigants did not appear in court nearly as often as these entries might lead one to suppose. See M. Hastings, as above, p. 102, note 41. But as litigation increased, so inevitably did the throng of litigants.

voked legislation to curb an intolerable importunity.[54] But the Commons, greatly to the advantage of husbandmen and yeomen of means, was fatally torn between a natural disposition to maintain a county suffrage restricted to men of quality, and an understandable desire to lighten the burden of the knight's wages by sharing it more widely.[55] Town Courts, if the experiences of Leicester and Northampton are anything to go by, were similarly afflicted at election time by mobs of unenfranchised inhabitants 'of little substance and of no discretion' asserting themselves indomitably and attempting to exercise an influence upon public life by voting.[56]

Perhaps the most continuous and enduring influence exerted by this emergent class of small farmers and artisans upon public life is to be found, however, neither in its clamorous subversion of the proprieties at election time, nor even in its moments of overwhelming violence during the Peasants' Revolt and Cade's Rebellion, when the established order of things was suddenly, though briefly, threatened with unimaginable horrors and annihilating disasters, but in religion: for the long history of English non-conformity began with those members of this obscure class who responded to the call of Lollardy even to the point of martyrdom.[57]

*　　　*　　　*

New forces threaten established classes and established usages in much the same way as new knowledge threatens established concepts and established assumptions. And the periods when such forces are working their way through the social system are easy neither for contemporaries nor indeed for those who come after and seek to understand what has happened. So far as the later Middle Ages are concerned, rooted prejudices redouble the difficulties of achieving such an understanding — the prejudice that

[54] Stubbs (op. cit., p. 103, note 42), pp. 265, 420, etc.

[55] L. C. Latham: The Collection of the Wages of the Knights of the Shire, E.H.R., Vol. 48 (1933), p. 459.

[56] V.C.H., Northants., Vol. III, p. 9.

[57] K. B. McFarlane: *John Wycliffe and the Beginnings of English Non-Conformity*, London, 1952.

strong and efficient government is necessarily better for society than government that is divided and ineffectual; the prejudice that the well-being of the highest class in the land is the surest touchstone of the prosperity of an age; the prejudice that output, not output per man, but sheer aggregate production of goods and services regardless of the cost at which it is achieved, is a sovereign good.

If we can rid ourselves of these illiberal shiboleths; if we can take our stand, not with Shakespeare, but with Hume and Macaulay, and value a period, politically and socially, not for the glamour and power of its dominant personalities nor even for the wealth and ostentation of its noble and gentle classes, but for its achievements in enlarging the range and enriching the quality of the freedom enjoyed by those who neither rule kingdoms nor control provinces, then perhaps we shall see the later Middle Ages in perspective, as a period of tremendous advance not only constitutionally, but also in social and economic affairs.

In these matters, as it may be in others, the true heir of the later Middle Ages was not the hectic age of the Tudors with its disastrous early Stuart epilogue, but those years of the later seventeenth and early eighteenth centuries when royal power was at last decisively curbed, and when another pause in the rate of population growth enabled real wages to rise quickly enough to provoke, once again, censorious comment upon the demoralizing self-indulgence of sections of the community which had been obliged to live far more soberly hitherto. Agriculture, industry, and distribution, all responded energetically to the challenge of this rising demand, and the domestic market was transformed by a rapid broadening of the range of things to buy and a rapid modernization of methods of retailing. And once again the import trade reflected the current trend: it was then, for example, that the ordinary Englishman acquired his abiding passion for tea.[58]

[58] D. Defoe: *The Complete English Tradesman*; R. Davis: English Foreign Trade 1660-1700, Ec.H.R., Second Series, Vol. VII, No. 2 (1954); A. H. John: Aspects of English Economic Growth in the First Half of the Eighteenth Century, *Economica*, May, 1961.

Resemblances between the later Middle Ages and the later seventeenth and early eighteenth centuries, however, if unmistakeable from certain points of view, must not be exaggerated. The developments of the later period were incomparably greater than those of the earlier one. And immeasurable things divided the world of Fortescue from the world of Defoe. But the seventeenth century built where the Middle Ages had sunk deep foundations; and it is, after all, first steps which are hardest to make and most interesting to recall and examine.

APPENDIX I[1]

CIVIC LOANS[2]

£'s

1377 — 1399		1413 — 1422		1432 — 1442	
Bristol	3033-6-8	Bristol	2569-6-8	Bristol	1500-6-0
Southampton	702-11-8	York	816-0-0	Norwich	400-1-0
Salisbury	600-0-0	Norwich	606-2-8	Coventry	200-1-0
York	536-0-0	Salisbury	378-13-4	Salisbury	190-0-0
Winchester	426-13-4	Southampton	350-7-5	York	145-0-5
Norwich	400-0-0	Coventry	302-13-4		

[1] I owe all the figures in this table to the generosity of Dr A. Steel who placed his notes unreservedly at my disposal.

[2] Provincial cities, not London; only the biggest contributors and selected years. After 1442 civic loans drop sharply; after mid-century they become meagre. The figures are total not annual ones and include individual as well as corporate loans, fictitious loans as well as genuine ones. For further details see A. Steel: *The Receipt of the Exchequer 1377-1485*. Cambridge, 1954. Dr Steel prints the most notable civic loans for 1422-32 on pp. 196-7.

THE TAXES OF 1334 AND 1524[1]

£'s

	1334[2]			1524[3]		
	Town	Country	%	Town	Country	%
Beds.	196	9825	2·0	33	871	3·8
Berks.	1140	13548	8·4	525	1125	46·7
Bucks.	312	9767	3·2	86	999	8·6
Cambs.	826	13830	6·0	166	948	17·5
Derby.	368	6227	5·9	37	523	7·1
Devon	1425	11566	12·3	744	3878	19·2
Dorset	700	11546	6·1	203	1679	12·1
Essex	261	18003	1·4	16	3483	6·2
Gloucs.	3097	19523	15·9	665	1932	34·4
Hants.	1806	14819	12·2	325	1807	18·0
Heref.	700	5454	12·8	142	407	34·9
Herts.	417	8620	4·8	130	1002	13·0
Hunts.	120	6230	1·9	47	821	5·7
Leics.	267	10707	2·5	104	1037	10·0
Lincs.	2556	43231	5·9	303	2799	10·8
Norfolk	2876	47951	6·0	1175	2811	41·8
Northants.	653	16237	4·0	136	1812	7·5
Notts.	711	8742	8·1	86	455	18·9
Oxon.	1177	18934	6·2	119	1143	10·4
Salop	1184	7849	15·1	114	433	26·3
Somerset	785	18926	4·1	216	3340	6·5
Staffs.	427	7789	5·5	31	608	5·1
Suffolk	1176	19673	6·0	552	3071	18·0
Surrey	573	7723	7·4	509	1317	38·6
Sussex	578	15590	3·7	141	2111	6·7
Warwicks.	1075	11169	9·6	533	762	69·9
Worcs.	200	6811	2·9	164	658	24·9
Yorks.	3942	33782	11·7	403	1790	22·5

[1] Certain counties have been left out—Cornwall and Kent because Stannary and Cinq Port exemptions make nonsense of the returns; Middlesex, Northumberland and Wiltshire for want of satisfactory records at one period or the other.

[2] These are figures of the total assessed value upon which taxes were levied. Owing to the differential rates imposed, it is impossible to use the actual tax assessments. See P.R.O. K.R. Misc. Book 7.

[3] These are figures of taxes paid. A few of the records of the first instalment of 1524 are missing and records of the second instalment of 1525 have been used instead. For all of them see P.R.O. E.179, *passim*.

APPENDIX III

SOME EXAMPLES OF URBAN CHANGE[1]

	1334 £'s	1524 £'s	Ratio
Abingdon	18	54	3
Aylesbury	13	37	3
Barnstaple	19	38	2
Basingstoke	12	65	5
Boston	110	73	—2
Bristol	220	465	2
Bury St Edmunds	24	194	8
Cambridge	47	97	2
Chichester	25	62	2·5
Colchester	26	216	8
Coventry	75	489	6
Dartmouth	19	40	2
Dorchester	9	77	8
Enfield	18	128	7
Exeter	41	385	9
Gloucester	54	134	2·5
Guildford	15	52	3
Hadleigh	13	106	8
Hertford	6	38	6
Hull	31	130	4
Ipswich	65	282	4
King's Lynn	77	268	3
Lavenham	10	180	18
Leicester	27	104	4
Lewes	4	43	10
Lincoln	100	125	1
Newbury	27	121	4
Northampton	27	91	3

[continued]

	1334 £'s	1524 £'s	Ratio
Norwich	95	749	8
Nottingham	35	55	1·5
Oxford	91	105	1
Peterborough	38	44	1
Reading	29	223	7
Salisbury	75	405	5·5
Shaftesbury	20	60	3
Southampton	51	101	2
Southwark	17	387	22
Taunton	10	45	4
Tavistock	9	32	3·5
Tiverton	2	53	26
Totnes	8	144	18
Warwick	19	15	1
Wells	19	61	3
Westminster	3	131	43
Winchester	63	86	1·5
Windsor	11	93	8
Worcester	20	164	8
Wycombe	9	45	5
Yarmouth	100	125	1
York	162	192	1

[1]These are figures of taxes paid. Villages like Hadleigh paid at a fifteenth instead of at a tenth. Such payments have been recalculated so as to bring them into line with other urban payments in 1334. The third column is simply a rough reckoning of the number of times the 1524 tax payments exceed or fall short of the 1334 one.

INDEX